Character and Self

Thoughts from Emerson, Shakespeare, and Other Poets and Writers

Character and Self

*Thoughts from Emerson, Shakespeare,
and Other Poets and Writers*

Edited and Annotated by
Ron McAdow

pHp
Personal History Press
Lincoln, Massachusetts

For everyone determined to learn their way through life.

ISBN 979-8-9877537-6-7

Library of Congress Control Number: 2026903847

pHp
Personal History Press
Lincoln, Massachusetts

Contents

Introduction

Character, the basis of self-respect, involves many aspects of personhood. Individuals with high character have challenging aspirations. They are cognizant of circumstances but resist limitations. They cultivate relationships and choose judicious responses to their feelings. They are disciplined in the use of resources available to them.

Ralph Waldo Emerson sought to understand character and what it means to be a person. Emerson loved Shakespeare. He wrote:

> Shakespeare read the hearts of men and women,
> their probity, and their second thought, and wiles;
> the wiles of innocence, and the transitions by which
> virtues and vices slide into their contraries. All the
> sweets and all the terrors of human lot lay in his
> mind as truly but as softly as the landscape lies on
> the eye. He is inconceivably wise.[1]

Shakespeare and Emerson will be read and valued while English is spoken and human dilemmas remain. Shakespeare's work foreshadowed the Enlightenment and Emerson's reflected its glow. Both writers had wisdom; neither spouted dogma. By expressing his thoughts and feelings through a galaxy of characters, Shakespeare approached human experience from many angles. Emerson was trained as a preacher, but he gave it up. As a lecturer and writer, he warned his audience that he did not dispense pat truth.

> Let me remind the reader that I am only an
> experimenter. Do not set the least value on what
> I do, or the least discredit on what I do not, as if
> I pretended to settle anything as true or false. I
> unsettle all things. No facts are to me sacred; none
> are profane; I simply experiment, an endless seeker,
> with no Past at my back.

---

1   *Representative Men,* Shakespeare; or, the Poet (RWE)

> No truth so sublime but it may be trivial tomorrow
> in the light of new thoughts.[1]

On some themes, Emerson's ideas held constant over time, while others changed as he aged. This book gathers Emerson's thoughts on topics pertaining to character and self, interweaves the words of his poet-hero Shakespeare and other writers, mostly his contemporaries, and concludes with a summary of the challenges we face in life and the balances we attempt.

In the footnotes, works by Emerson, Shakespeare, and Walt Whitman are identfied by their initials: RWE, WS, and WW.

In one of the passages quoted below, Margaret Fuller wrote, "By Man I mean both man and woman." So did Emerson.

---

1   *Essays,* Circles (RWE)

Aspirations

Character

Emerson observed that our evaluation of the characters of other people is automatic and continuous.

> We are all discerners of spirits. That diagnosis lies aloft in our life or unconscious power, not in the understanding. The whole intercourse of society, its trade, its religion, its friendships, its quarrels, is one wide, judicial investigation of character. In full court, or in small committee, or confronted face to face, accuser and accused, men offer themselves to be judged. Against their will they exhibit those decisive trifles by which character is read.[1]

Emerson made many remarks about character, such as,

> The progress of every earnest mind flows from character, that sublime health which values one moment as another, and makes us great in all conditions, and is the only definition we have of freedom and power.[2]

Character is not literally the only definition we have of freedom and power. Emerson often used hyperbole. He could have written, "Character is the most important form of freedom and power" but he chose the stronger expression.

Both Emerson and the American poet Walt Whitman thought that character projects itself nonverbally.

> Character, — a reserved force which acts directly by presence.[3]

> (I and mine do not convince by arguments, similes, rhymes,
>   We convince by our presence.)[4]

---

1 *Essays,* The Oversoul (RWE)
2 *Society and Solitude,* Works and Days (RWE)
3 *Essays: Second Series,* Character (RWE)
4 *Leaves of Grass,* Song of the Open Road (WW)

Strong character implies a steady internal balance.

> The face which character wears to me is self-
> sufficingness. …Character is centrality, the
> impossibility of being displaced or overset.[1]

The impossibility of being overset suggests the ability to keep one's mental center of gravity over the legs of one's behavior. Whitman's soul *poised on itself.*

> O the joy of my soul leaning pois'd on itself,
> receiving identity through materials and loving
> them,
> observing characters and absorbing them.[2]

We can judge how central the idea of character was to Emerson by its treatment in many essays over many years. He noted that character is a quality that enables you to encounter life as it comes. He also wrote that persons of fine character and attitude can be thought of as the natural nobility, a class without reference to heredity, wealth, or social standing.

> There are graces in the demeanor of a polished
> and noble person, which are lost upon the eye of a
> churl. These are like the stars whose light has not
> yet reached us.[3]

We are all to some degree churlish—oblivious to the graces of others that we ought to perceive.

Ethics

Most people share basic ethical aspirations, including kindness and fairness. The application of these principles can be difficult. Neither Shakespeare nor Emerson thought that moral behavior could be defined without respect to circumstances. In *Romeo and Juliet,* Shakespeare has a wise friar say,

---

1   *Essays: Second Series,* Character (RWE)
2   *Leaves of Grass,* A Song of Joys (WW)
3   *Essays,* Spiritual Laws (RWE)

> Virtue itself turns vice, being misapplied;
> And vice sometimes by action dignified.[1]

Emerson separated morality from specific codes. *Obey your moral perceptions at this hour.*

> The cure for false theology is motherwit. Forget
> your books and traditions, and obey your moral
> perceptions at this hour. That which is signified
> by the words "moral " and "spiritual," is a lasting
> essence, and, with whatever illusions we have
> loaded them, will certainly bring back the words,
> age after age, to their ancient meaning.[2]

> What is moral? It is the respecting in action catholic
> or universal ends. Hear the definition which Kant
> gives of moral conduct: "Act always so that
> the immediate motive of thy will may become a
> universal rule for all intelligent beings."[3]

Emerson and most of his fellow Concordians sprang from Puritan stock and attended the church founded by their Puritan forebearers.

> Self-accusation, remorse, and the didactic morals
> of self-denial and strife with sin, is a view we are
> constrained by our constitution to take of the fact
> seen from the platform of action; but seen from the
> platform of intellection, there is nothing for us but
> praise and wonder.[4]

The *constitution* he refers to, that requires *self-accusation and remorse,* is the Puritan heritage. Without denying that he himself is rooted in that culture, he asserts that his view of human nature has lost its concern with a sinful fall.

---

1   *Romeo and Juliet,* Act II, Scene 3 (WS)
2   *Conduct of Life,* Worship (RWE)
3   *Society and Solitude,* Civilization (RWE)
4   *Addresses,* Method of Nature (RWE)

The principle of fair play is basic. If it's not fair, it's not right. And yet even this branch of virtuous living is complex. We construe fair behavior with reasonable clarity as individual teachers, parents, or referees—but it is more difficult to feel comfortable about the fairness of the groups we inhabit. Groups containing fair-minded individuals have been grossly unfair towards persons of other races. We accept privileges that come to us for reasons other than merit (although we are adept at figuring out why we deserve these good things). With respect to the environment, we continue individual behaviors known, cumulatively, to be destructive to wildlife, to ecosystems, and to cause climate change. We want to be responsible, but still, for the most part, we guide our behavior by that of the people around us. We don't want to be oddballs—we want to be normal.

In *Measure for Measure*, Shakespeare's young protagonist is condemned to death—by sudden strict enforcement of a long-neglected law— for having impregnated his fiancée. The young man's friend, Escalus, pleads for leniency: perhaps the (evil) acting governor, Angelo, had himself committed a similar offence? Angelo argues that fairness lies in impartial application of the written law.

> **Angelo.** 'Tis one thing to be tempted, Escalus
> Another thing to fall. I not deny,
> The jury, passing on the prisoner's life,
> May in the sworn twelve have a thief or two
> Guiltier than him they try.
> What's open made to justice,
> That justice seizes: what know the laws
> That thieves do pass on thieves? 'Tis very pregnant,
> The jewel that we find, we stoop and take't
> Because we see it; but what we do not see
> We tread upon, and never think of it.
> You may not so extenuate his offence
> For I have had such faults; but rather tell me,
> When I, that censure him, do so offend,

Let mine own judgment pattern out my death,
And nothing come in partial. Sir, he must die.
Escalus. *[Aside]* Well, heaven forgive him! and
forgive us all!
Some rise by sin, and some by virtue fall.[1]

Escalus has a good character, which Angelo lacks. Are people basically good or bad? In addressing that question, Emerson referred to Greek mythology.

Too good for banning, and too bad for blessing, it reminds us of a tradition of the pagan mythology, in any attempt to settle its character. 'I overheard Jove,[2] one day,' said Silenus[3], 'talking of destroying the earth; he said, it had failed; they were all rogues and vixens, who went from bad to worse, as fast as the days succeeded each other. Minerva said, she hoped not; they were only ridiculous little creatures, with this odd circumstance, that they had a blur, or indeterminate aspect, seen far or seen near; if you called them bad, they would appear so; if you called them good, they would appear so; and there was no one person or action among them, which would not puzzle her owl, much more all Olympus, to know whether it was fundamentally bad or good.'[4]

All good-hearted people aim for an upright character and decent ethical values. A humble Shakespearian shepherd offered a common-sense formula for virtuous living.

Sir, I am a true labourer: I earn that I eat, get that I wear; owe no man hate, envy no man's happiness; glad of other men's good, content with my harm;

---

1 *Measure for Measure,* Act II, Scene 1 (WS)
2 Emerson used the Roman names for the gods, even when he was referring to ancient Greece. "Jove" was Zeus; "Minerva" was Athena.
3 Silenus is a unique figure in Greek mythology. He is portrayed as a drunken wise man.
4 *Essays: Second Series,* Manners (RWE)

> and the greatest of my pride is to see my ewes
> graze and my lambs suck.[1]

Touchstone, the clown in *As You Like It,* pronounced the shepherd a natural philosopher. No doubt Emerson agreed and loved that exchange. But Emerson never construed virtuous behavior as simple. Ideals change; future right offends present right and vice-versa.

> With eyes open, he makes the choice of virtue,
> which outrages the virtuous; of religion, which
> churches stop their discords to burn and
> exterminate; for the highest virtue is always
> against the law.[2]

The poet Emily Dickinson[3] made a similar point.

> Much Madness is divinest Sense –
> To a discerning Eye –
> Much Sense – the starkest Madness
> 'Tis the Majority
> In this, as all, prevail –
> Assent – and you are sane –
> Demur – you're straightway dangerous –
> And handled with a Chain – [4]

Is it exaggeration to write that dissenters are "handled with a chain"? Or that "the highest virtue is always against the law"? Maybe. But for long years of Dickinson's and Emerson's lives it was illegal to assist people fleeing enslavement. Emerson praised *acts of justice.*

> We have a debt to every great heart, to every fine
> genius; to those who have put life and fortune on
> the cast of an act of justice; to those who have

---

1   *As You Like It,* Act III, Scene 2 (WS)
2   *Conduct of Life,* Worship (RWE)
3   Dickinson's life overlapped with Emerson's—but her poems were not published until after their deaths.
4   *Much Madness is divinest Sense,* Emily Dickinson

added new sciences; to those who have refined life
by elegant pursuits.[1]

A person who "put life and fortune on the cast of an act
of justice" is Lydia Maria Child (1802-1880), author of a best
seller entitled *The American Frugal Housewife*. Her outspoken
dedication to the abolition of slavery cost her publishers
and popularity, but she never wavered. In the 1840s, Child
criticized Emerson's relative standoffishness in denouncing
slavery—he did not wish to be identified with any single cause.
Emerson later became vocal about this evil but he never paid
the personal price that Child did. Emerson was aware of Child's
sacrifices when he wrote the lines above.

We have on the one hand custom and convention, and on
the other, free-thinking individualism. Society's slowly evolving
mores vs. individual impulses and beliefs. A Shakespearean
character declares himself independent of convention.

> Thou, Nature, art my goddess; to thy law
> My services are bound. Wherefore should I
> Stand in the plague of custom.[2]

For free-thinkers, custom and convention are anathema.

> Society will pardon much to genius and special
> gifts, but, being in its nature a convention, it loves
> what is conventional, or what belongs to coming
> together.[3]

Our reflex is to apply *conventional* to ideas or behaviors that
we regard as shallow or outdated, whereas *coming together* has a
positive ring to it, a need-filling joining of hands. The counter-
culture of my youth wanted everyone to *come together* but not
to be bound by convention. Although we rejected conventional
materialism, racism, and sexism, we expected conformity to
new norms.

---

1   *Conduct of Life*, Considerations by the Way (RWE)
2   *King Lear*, Act I, Scene 2 (WS)
3   *Essays: Second Series*, Manners (RWE)

> Every man should call the institutions of society
> to account, and examine their fitness to him.... Is
> our housekeeping sacred and honorable? Does it
> raise and inspire us, or does it cripple us instead?
> We spend our incomes for paint and paper, for a
> hundred trifles, I know not what, and not for the
> things of a man. Our expense is almost all for
> conformity. It is for cake that we run in debt; 't
> is not the intellect, not the heart, not beauty, not
> worship, that costs so much. Why needs any man
> be rich? [1]

A manifesto for the hippies, truly—and for his young friend Henry David Thoreau.

Does *wickedness* have a social function?

> It is an esoteric doctrine of society, that a little
> wickedness is good to make muscle; as if
> conscience were not good for hands and legs, as
> if poor decayed formalists of law and order cannot
> run like wild goats, wolves, and conies; that, as
> there is a use in medicine for poisons, so the world
> cannot move without rogues; that public spirit
> and the ready hand are as well found among the
> malignants. 'Tis not very rare, the coincidence of
> sharp private and political practice, with public
> spirit, and good neighborhood. [2]
>
> Why exaggerate the power of virtue? Why be an
> angel before your time? [3]

Though he asked such questions, Emerson, in the end, preached virtue.

> So much benevolence as a man hath, so much life
> hath he.
> When in innocency, or when by intellectual
> perception, he attains to say, — 'I love the Right;
> Truth is beautiful within and without, forevermore.

---

1   *Addresses,* Man the Reformer (RWE)
2   *Conduct of Life,* Power (RWE)
3   *Representative Men,* Montaigne; or, the Skeptic (RWE)

> Virtue, I am thine: save me: use me: thee will I
> serve, day and night, in great, in small, that I may
> be not virtuous, but virtue;' — then is the end of the
> creation answered, and God is well pleased. [1]

Emerson's "Divinity School Address," which he gave at Harvard in 1838, included the foregoing, which seems tame enough, but that lecture also criticized ministers who preached conventional doctrine without challenging their congregations to higher moral attainment. His words angered the faculty, and Emerson was not invited to speak again at Harvard until 1868.

Here is Emerson's challenge to young adults:

> I will not dissemble my hope, that each person
> whom I address has felt his own call to cast aside
> all evil customs, timidities, and limitations, and to
> be in his place a free and helpful man, a reformer,
> a benefactor, not content to slip along through
> the world like a footman or a spy, escaping by his
> nimbleness and apologies as many knocks as he
> can, but a brave and upright man, who must find
> or cut a straight road to everything excellent in the
> earth, and not only go honorably himself, but make
> it easier for all who follow him, to go in honor and
> with benefit.[2]

Though he clung to his ideals, Emerson had reservations about *ideologues*.

> Those, who are urging with most ardor what are
> called the greatest benefits of mankind, are narrow,
> self-pleasing, conceited men, and affect us as the
> insane do.[3]

> The criticism and attack on institutions which we
> have witnessed, has made one thing plain, that
> society gains nothing whilst a man, not himself
> renovated, attempts to renovate things around him:
> he has become tediously good in some particular,

---

1 *Addresses,* The Divinity School Address (RWE)
2 *Addresses,* Man the Reformer (RWE)
3 *Addresses,* Lecture on the Times (RWE)

but negligent or narrow in the rest; and hypocrisy
and vanity are often the disgusting result.[1]

Walt Whitman also sounded this theme:

> What blurt is this about virtue and about vice?
>   Evil propels me and reform of evil propels me, I
> stand indifferent.[2]

So did Virginia Woolf, who had Mrs. Dalloway complain,

> Miss Kilman would do anything for the Russians,
> starved herself for the Austrians, but in private
> inflicted positive torture, so insensitive was she…
> she was never in the room five minutes without
> making you feel her superiority, your inferiority; how
> poor she was; how rich you were; how she lived
> in a slum without a cushion or a bed or a rug or
> whatever it might be, all her soul rusted with that
> grievance sticking in it.[3]

Courage

Steadfast resolution in the face of disapproval or danger is
the virtue we call *courage*.

> In regard to disagreeable and formidable things,
> prudence does not consist in evasion, or in flight,
> but in courage. He who wishes to walk in the most
> peaceful parts of life with any serenity, must screw
> himself up to resolution.[4]

Peace with yourself requires the courage to stand your own
ground. Only by this forthrightness do you earn the right to the
serenity of self-respect—so argues Emerson, but he allows:

> Each has his own courage, as his own talent; but
> the courage of the tiger is one, and of the horse
> another. The dog that scorns to fight, will fight

---

1 *Essays: Second Series,* New England Reformers (RWE)
2 *Leaves of Grass,* Song of Myself (WW)
3 *Mrs. Dalloway,* Virginia Woolf
4 *Essays,* Prudence (RWE)

for his master. The llama that will carry a load if you caress him, will refuse food and die if he is scourged. The fury of onset is one, and of calm endurance another. There is a courage of the cabinet as well as a courage of the field; a courage of manners in private assemblies, and another in public assemblies; a courage which enables one man to speak masterly to a hostile company, whilst another man who can easily face a cannon's mouth dares not open his own.

Social courage and physical courage—each is admirable. The exercise of social courage—readiness to express a view known to be unpopular with your company—was often lived by Emerson. And he knew the perpetual tension between candid expression and social grace, which leaves the decision of when to speak and when to hold your peace ever in doubt. Physical courage is a simpler matter, rarely tested in literary persons, but a fond topic of their imaginings. Rudyard Kipling's, for example:

> "What dam of lances brought thee forth to jest at the dawn with Death?"
> Lightly answered the Colonel's son: "I hold by the blood of my clan."
> "Take up the mare for my father's gift—by God, she has carried a man!"[1]

Emerson thought that danger inspires some individuals to their highest self-realization.

> Courage [is] the perfect will, which no terrors can shake, which is attracted by frowns or threats or hostile armies, nay, needs these to awake and fan its reserved energies into a pure flame, and is never quite itself until the hazard is extreme; then it is serene and fertile, and all its powers play well.
>
> Animal resistance, the instinct of the animal when cornered, is no doubt common; but the pure article,

---

1   *The Ballad of East and West,* Rudyard Kipling

> courage with eyes, courage with conduct, self-
> possession at the cannon's mouth, cheerfulness in
> lonely adherence to the right, is the endowment of
> elevated characters. I need not show how much it is
> esteemed, for the people give it the first rank. They
> forgive everything to it. [1]

Who does not wonder, from time to time, how they would fare if their courage was put to the test? We bend the knee to the firefighters who, on 9/11, climbed the steps of the remaining tower, knowing that the first had collapsed. People in the military and in public safety have need for this intrepid grit.

Emerson linked courage to cheerfulness.

> That which befits us, embosomed in beauty and
> wonder as we are, is cheerfulness and courage, and
> the endeavor to realize our aspirations. [2]

In Shakespeare's world, courage and honor were close kin. For some of his characters, honor was the supreme and indispensable distinction.

> Set honour in one eye and death i' the other,
> And I will look on both indifferently,
> For let the gods so speed me as I love
> The name of honour more than I fear death. [3]

Falstaff, the chubby merry rogue who appeared in several of Shakespeare's plays, placed no value on honor. His former friend and drinking companion, Prince Henry, chided Falstaff's reluctance to join in battle.

> **Prince Henry.** Thou owest God a death.
> **Falstaff.** 'Tis not due yet; I would be loath to pay
> him before his day.
> What need I be so forward with him that calls not on
> me?

---

1   *Society and Solitude,* Courage (RWE)
2   *Essays: Second Series,* New England Reformers (RWE)
3   *Julius Caesar,* Act I Scene 2 (WS)

Well, 'tis no matter; honour pricks me on. Yea, but
how if honour prick me off when I come on? how
then? Can honour set to a leg? no: or an arm? no:
or take away the grief of a wound? no.
Honour hath no skill in surgery, then? no.
What is honour? a word.
What is in that word honour? What is that honour?
Air.
A trim reckoning! Who hath it? He that died o'
Wednesday.
Doth he feel it? no. Doth he hear it? no.
'Tis insensible, then. Yea, to the dead.
But will it not live with the living?
No. Why? detraction will not suffer it.
Therefore I'll none of it.
Honour is a mere scutcheon:[1] and so ends my
catechism.[2]

Tranquility of Soul

Without rejecting practical values, Emerson spoke for a rich
inner life and tranquility of the soul.

We live on different planes or platforms. There is an
external life, which is educated at school, taught
to read, write, cipher, and trade; taught to grasp all
the boy can get, urging him to put himself forward,
to make himself useful and agreeable in the world,
to ride, run, argue, and contend, unfold his talents,
shine, conquer, and possess.

But the inner life sits at home, and does not learn
to do things, nor value these feats at all. 'Tis a
quiet, wise perception. It loves truth, because it is
itself real; it loves right, it knows nothing else: but it
makes no progress; was as wise in our first memory
of it as now; is just the same now in maturity and
hereafter in age, it was in youth. We have grown
to manhood and womanhood; we have powers,
connection, children, reputations, professions: this
makes no account of them all. It lives in the great

---

1   A "scutcheon" is a useless decoration.
2   *Henry IV Part 1*, Act V Scene 1 (WS)

present; it makes the present great. This tranquil, well-founded, wide seeing soul is no express-rider, no attorney, no magistrate: it lies in the sun, and broods on the world.[1]

Emerson used the word *soul* in more than one way.

I see, that when souls reach a certain clearness of perception, they accept a knowledge and motive above selfishness. A breath of will blows eternally through the universe of souls in the direction of the Right and Necessary. It is the air which all intellects inhale and exhale, and it is the wind which blows the worlds into order and orbit.[2]

The paragraph above moves from the sense of soul as the spiritual identity of each person to a different meaning: a *universe of souls.*

Within man is the soul of the whole; the wise silence; the universal beauty, to which every part and particle is equally related; the eternal ONE. And this deep power in which we exist, and whose beatitude is all accessible to us, is not only self-sufficing and perfect in every hour, but the act of seeing, and the thing seen, the seer and the spectacle, the subject and the object, are one. We see the world piece by piece, as the sun, the moon, the animal, the tree; but the whole, of which these are the shining parts, is the soul.[3]

In the Christian world of his time, this was a radical stance, and it was controversial, but Emerson's kindliness, his conventional mode of living, and his dignity preserved his reputation. His lectures continued to attract paying audiences. Walt Whitman's lifestyle was more nonconforming than Emerson's, but Whitman made and kept his place among American poets. He, too, used *soul* in an expansive sense.

---

1   *Society and Solitude,* Success (RWE)
2   *Conduct of Life,* Fate (RWE)
3   *Essays,* The Oversoul (RWE)

Beautiful world of new superber birth that rises to
my eyes,
  Like a limitless golden cloud filling the western
sky,
    Emblem of general maternity lifted above all,
    Sacred shape of the bearer of daughters and sons,
    Out of thy teeming womb thy giant babes in
ceaseless procession issuing,
    Acceding from such gestation, taking and giving
continual strength and life,
    World of the real — world of the twain in one,
    World of the soul, born by the world of the real
alone, led to identity, body, by it alone,
    Yet in beginning only, incalculable masses of
composite precious materials,
    By history's cycles forwarded, by every nation,
language, hither sent,
    Ready, collected here, a freer, vast, electric world,
to be constructed here,
    (The true New World, the world of orbic science,
morals, literatures to come,)
    Thou wonder world yet undefined, unform'd,
neither do I define thee,
    How can I pierce the impenetrable blank of the
future?[1]

Falstaff's soul was something he could mortgage for
present financial benefit.

> **Falstaff.** I am damned in hell for swearing to
> gentlemen my friends, you were good soldiers and
> tall fellows; and when Mistress Bridget lost the
> handle of her fan, I took't upon mine honour thou
> hadst it not.
> **Pistol.** Didst not thou share? hadst thou not fifteen
> pence?
> **Falstaff.** Reason, you rogue, reason: thinkest thou
> I'll endanger my soul gratis?[2]

---

1   *Leaves of Grass,* Thou Mother with Thy Equal Brood (WW)
2   *Merry Wives of Windsor,* Act II Scene 2 (WS)

Emerson valued his soul in a more serious sense.

> The soul knows only the soul. All else is idle weeds
> for her wearing.
> After its own law and not by arithmetic is the
> rate of its progress to be computed. The soul's
> advances are not made by gradation, such as
> can be represented by motion in a straight line;
> but rather by ascension of state, such as can
> be represented by metamorphosis… With each
> divine impulse the mind rends the thin rinds of
> the visible and finite, and comes out into eternity,
> and inspires and expires its air. It converses with
> truths that have always been spoken in the world,
> and becomes conscious of a closer sympathy with
> Zeno and Arrian[1], than with persons in the house.[2]

Genuine and Grounded

The expression, "He's an old soul" is common in conversation. We apply it to a person who is both *genuine* and *grounded*. We can rely on the integrity of a *genuine* individual. We use the word *grounded* to describe people who speak and behave from their authentic selves; they are in touch with both inward and outward reality. One of Shakespeare's protagonists was a duke whose enemies had forced him and his followers to live in the forest. The duke, a well-grounded man, makes this argument to his friends:

> Are not these woods
> More free from peril than the envious court?
> Here feel we not the penalty of Adam,
> The seasons' difference; as the icy fang
> And churlish chiding of the winter's wind,
> Which when it bites and blows upon my body,
> Even till I shrink with cold,

---

1 Zeno of Citium was a Hellenistic philosopher from Cyprus and the founder of the Stoic school of philosophy. He taught in Athens from about 300 BCE. Arrian was a Greek historian, philosopher, and statesman who lived in the 2nd century CE.

2 *Essays*, The Oversoul (RWE)

I smile and say 'This is no flattery; these are counsellors
That feelingly persuade me what I am.'[1]

Walt Whitman published a letter from Emerson at the front of the second edition of his book of poems. It began: "—I am not blind to the worth of the wonderful gift of *Leaves of Grass*. I find it the most extraordinary piece of wit and wisdom that America has yet contributed." Although the context of the following paragraph was not literally an endorsement of Whitman, it might as well have been. It followed, by a few years, the publication of *Leaves of Grass*.

I look upon the simple and childish virtues of veracity and honesty as the root of all that is sublime in character. Speak as you think, be what you are, pay your debts of all kinds. I prefer to be owned as sound and solvent, and my word as good as my bond, and to be what cannot be skipped, or dissipated, or undermined, to all the *éclat* in the universe. This reality is the foundation of friendship, religion, poetry, and art. At the top or at the bottom of all illusions, I set the cheat which still leads us to work and live for appearances, in spite of our conviction, in all sane hours, that it is what we really are that avails with friends, with strangers, and with fate or fortune.[2]

Emerson thought this quality defined a gentleman.

The gentleman is a man of truth, lord of his own actions, and expressing that lordship in his behavior, not in any manner dependent and servile either on persons, or opinions, or possessions.[3]

Today we would eliminate the gender reference. What would we say instead of *the gentleman*? The *person of distinguished dignity*?

---

1   *As You Like It*, Act II, Scene 1 (WS)
2   *Conduct of Life*, Illusions (RWE)
3   *Essays: Second Series*, Manners (RWE)

In the same essay, Emerson expanded on the quality of groundedness.

> We are such lovers of self-reliance, that we excuse in a man many sins, if he will show us a complete satisfaction in his position, which asks no leave to be, of mine, or any man's good opinion.[1]

> The hero is he who is immovably centred. The main difference between people seems to be, that one man can come under obligations on which you can rely, — is obligable; and another is not.[2]

From there he passes to a more abstract level, with his distinctly Emersonian expression of the Eastern religious image of individual participation in the universal divinity.

> We cannot bandy words with nature, or deal with her as we deal with persons. If we measure our individual forces against hers, we may easily feel as if we were the sport of an insuperable destiny. But if, instead of identifying ourselves with the work, we feel that the soul of the workman streams through us, we shall find the peace of the morning dwelling first in our hearts, and the fathomless powers of gravity and chemistry, and, over them, of life, preexisting within us in their highest form.[3]

This is not theology because Emerson did not offer it as a statement of fact or as an unevidenced hypothesis to be accepted on faith. He posed a choice about how to think; about how to tune our imaginations. "If we *feel* that the soul of the workman…" What is *the work*? The physical world we experience. *The workman* is the force and process of creation. By conceiving our inner selves as participating in this mysterious fountain, *we shall find the peace of the morning* in our hearts. This is a state of mind we may aspire to. Although few of us can

---

1   *Essays: Second Series,* Manners
2   *Conduct of Life,* Considerations by the Way
3   *Essays: Second Series,* Nature (RWE)

remain in that mental place for long, it is an imaginative act we can practice.

We know that we present preferred and less preferred versions of ourselves in different times and circumstances. Emerson warned us of our transparency.

> Character is always known. The least admixture of a lie, — for example, the taint of vanity, the least attempt to make a good impression, a favorable appearance, — will instantly vitiate the effect. But speak the truth, and all nature and all spirits help you with unexpected furtherance.[1]

Our aspiration to be grounded segues into our wish to be genuine.

> The first point of courtesy must always be truth, as really all the forms of good-breeding point that way.[2]

> All rests at last on that integrity which dwarfs talent, and can spare it.
> A man who is sure of his point, carries a broad and contented expression, which everybody reads. And you cannot rightly train one to an air and manner, except by making him the kind of man of whom that manner is the natural expression. Nature forever puts a premium on reality. What is done for effect, is seen to be done for effect; what is done for love, is felt to be done for love.[3]

> Sincerity is more excellent than flattery. Deal so plainly with man and woman, as to constrain the utmost sincerity, and destroy all hope of trifling with you. It is the highest compliment you can pay.[4]

This is easily swallowed because *flattery* has a negative sound. But no one receives as much appreciation as they wish

---

1   *Addresses,* The Divinity School Address (RWE)
2   *Essays: Second Series,* Manners (RWE)
3   *Conduct of Life,* Considerations by the Way (RWE)
4   *Essays,* Oversoul (RWE)

for and deserve. If I emphasize the positive to my companions, and keep reservations to myself, I cannot claim "the utmost sincerity." We make our own choices. Usually when we speak of flattery, we mean self-serving falsehood. In the first scene of *The Tragedy of King Lear*, the King poses this question to his daughters:

> Which of you shall we say doth love us most?
> That we our largest bounty may extend
> Where nature doth with merit challenge.

Lear's eldest daughter, Goneral, replies,

> Sir, I love you more than words can wield the
> matter;
> Dearer than eyesight, space, and liberty;
> Beyond what can be valued, rich or rare;
> No less than life, with grace, health, beauty,
> honour;
> As much as child e'er lov'd, or father found;
> A love that makes breath poor, and speech unable.
> Beyond all manner of so much I love you.

Hearing this, her sister Cordelia addresses the audience:

> What shall Cordelia speak? Love, and be silent.

Lear's second daughter, Regan, tells her father,

> Sir, I am made
> Of the selfsame metal that my sister is,
> And prize me at her worth.
> In my true heart I find she names my very deed of
> love;
> Only she comes too short, that I profess
> Myself an enemy to all other joys
> Which the most precious square of sense
> possesses,
> And find I am alone felicitate
> In your dear Highness' love.

Finally, Lear turns to the youngest of the three, unmarried Cordelia, who responds with candor.

> Good my lord,
> You have begot me, bred me, lov'd me; I
> Return those duties back as are right fit,
> Obey you, love you, and most honour you.
> Why have my sisters husbands, if they say
> They love you all? Haply, when I shall wed,
> That lord whose hand must take my plight shall carry
> Half my love with him, half my care and duty.
> Sure I shall never marry like my sisters,
> To love my father all.

Cordelia's refusal to compete in exaggerated protestations of love infuriates Lear.

> **Lear.** So young, and so untender?
> **Cordelia.** So young, my lord, and true.
> **Lear.** Let it be so! thy truth then be thy dower!
> For, by the sacred radiance of the sun,
> The mysteries of Hecate and the night;
> By all the operation of the orbs
> From whom we do exist and cease to be;
> Here I disclaim all my paternal care,
> Propinquity and property of blood,
> And as a stranger to my heart and me
> Hold thee from this for ever.

Cordelia pleads her sincerity.

> If for I want that glib and oily art
> To speak and purpose not, since what I well intend,
> I'll do't before I speak.

Her reasoning is to no avail. Later in the act the older sisters reveal their true opinion of their father.

> **Goneril.** You see how full of changes his age is. The observation we have made of it hath not been little.

> He always lov'd our sister most, and with what
> poor judgment he hath now cast her off appears
> too grossly.
> **Regan.** 'Tis the infirmity of his age; yet he hath
> ever but slenderly known himself.
> **Goneril.** The best and soundest of his time hath
> been but rash; then must we look to receive from
> his age, not alone the imperfections of long-
> ingraffed condition, but therewithal the unruly
> waywardness that infirm and choleric years bring
> with them.

Thus they spoke at the end of Act I. Their machinations and their father's receptiveness to their bait set up four subsequent acts of plotting, violence, and death. If Lear had seen through Goneril and Regan's base flattery and valued Cordelia's candor at its true worth, what then? No play—and no lesson from Shakespeare about the danger of taking flattery at face value.

Capacities

> Power dwells with cheerfulness; hope puts us in a
> working mood, whilst despair is no muse, and un-
> tunes the active powers.[1]

Power is in this sentence twice. Not political power but interior power—the sense in which Emerson most frequently uses this word—referring to a personal capacity to deliver clear thought, precise expression, and effective action. A cheerful attitude both results from, and prepares the way for, such results. Cheer and internal power connect with motivation to generate enthusiasm.

> Nothing great was ever achieved without
> enthusiasm.[2]

---

1   *Conduct of Life,* Culture (RWE)
2   *Essays,* Circles (RWE)

Does enthusiasm happen to us? Or does it gush from our inherent temperaments? What can generate this positive force?

> The Greeks fabled that Venus[1] was born of the foam of the sea. Nothing interests us which is stark or bounded, but only what streams with life, what is an act or endeavor to reach somewhat beyond.[2]

Emerson intends that his own writing both *stream with life* and *reach somewhat beyond.* (In the usage of Emerson's era, *somewhat* meant *something.*) This defines two categories for subjects of interest to human beings. What streams with life? The allusion to Venus points to sexuality—which, biologically speaking, is certainly an endeavor to reach beyond. And Venus belongs to the world of mythology—a story realm that has stood the test of time, and that reaches beyond objective reality into imagination.

No activity inherently streams with life. Our excitement wells up, or our ennui pulls the plug, depending on our temperament and mood.

> With adults, as with children, one class enter cordially into the game, and whirl with the whirling world; the others have cold hands, and remain bystanders; or are only dragged in by the humor and vivacity of those who can carry a dead weight.[3]

Enthusiasm (*enthousiasme*) was an important word for Madame de Staël.[4]

> Many people are prejudiced against enthusiasm. They confuse it with fanaticism, and this is a great mistake. Fanaticism is an exclusive passion whose object is an opinion. Enthusiasm is concerned with

---

1 The Greeks called her Aphrodite
2 *Conduct of Life,* Beauty (RWE)
3 *Conduct of Life,* Power (RWE)
4 Anne Louise Germaine de Staël-Holstein, commonly referred to as Madame de Staël, was a gifted pan-European intellectual and writer, a champion of freedom and a nemesis of Napoleon. She was of great importance to Emerson and his contemporaries.

> universal harmony; it is the love of the beautiful,
> the elevation of the soul, and the enjoyment of
> self-sacrifice all combined into one sentiment that
> has grandeur and tranquility. The meaning of this
> word among the Greeks is the noblest definition
> of it: enthusiasm means God in us. Indeed,
> when man's life is emotionally overflowing it has
> something of the divine.
> Everything that leads us to sacrifice our own
> comfort or life is almost always related to
> enthusiasm. For the direct route of selfish reason
> must be to regard one's self as the object of all
> one's efforts and to value nothing in the world but
> health, wealth, and power.[1]

There are many kinds of power. Shakespeare's Cleopatra had notable personal power.

> Age cannot wither her, nor custom stale
> Her infinite variety: other women cloy
> The appetites they feed: but she makes hungry
> Where most she satisfies; for vilest things
> Become themselves in her.[2]

In the play, Cleopatra sought to use her personal force to maintain political power. She wanted to remain a queen. Human ambitions are not limited to spiritual and interpersonal attainments. People also seek worldly power— strength that comes with rank and position. Economic power offers freedoms and opportunities. Practical achievements bring status and applause.

> Men admire the man who can organize their
> wishes and thoughts in stone and wood and steel
> and brass, — the man who can build the boat, who
> has the impiety to make the rivers run the way he
> wants them, who can lead his telegraph through
> the ocean from shore to shore; who, sitting in his

---

1 *Madame de Staël on Politics, Literature, and National Character,* Madame de Stael

2 *Antony and Cleopatra,* Act II, Scene 2 (WS)

closet, can lay out the plans of a campaign, — sea-war and land-war; such that the best generals and admirals, when all is done, see that they must thank him for success.[1]

If a man can raise a small city to be a great kingdom, can make bread cheap, can irrigate deserts, can join oceans by canals, can subdue steam, can organize victory, can lead the opinions of mankind, can enlarge knowledge, 'tis no matter whether his nose is parallel to his spine, as it ought to be, or whether he has a nose at all; whether his legs are straight, or whether his legs are amputated; his deformities will come to be reckoned ornamental, and advantageous on the whole.[2]

Although Emerson did not hesitate to acknowledge material achievements, he most often praised success in spirit, intellect, and attitude.

They are the kings of the world who give the color of their present thought to all nature and all art, and persuade men by the cheerful serenity of their carrying the matter, that this thing which they do, is the apple which the ages have desired to pluck, now at last ripe and inviting nations to the harvest. The great man makes the great thing. ... The day is always his, who works in it with serenity and great aims.[3]

The expansive Whitman sounded his bugle for interior force and conquest.

O while I live to be the ruler of life, not a slave,
    To meet life as a powerful conqueror,
    No fumes, no ennui, no more complaints or
scornful criticisms,
    To these proud laws of the air, the water and the
ground, proving my interior soul impregnable,

---

1   *Society and Solitude,* Courage (RWE)
2   *Conduct of Life,* Beauty (RWE)
3   *Addresses,* The American Scholar (RWE)

> And nothing exterior shall ever take command of
> me.[1]

Personal force aims to bring success in some realm or other. There is no guarantee that effort, even effort long sustained, will attain its goal. In that case consolation comes from a well-earned self-judgment.

> I look on that man as happy, who, when there
> is question of success, looks into his work for a
> reply, not into the market, not into opinion, not into
> patronage. In every variety of human employment,
> in the mechanical and in the fine arts, in navigation,
> in faring, in legislating, there are among the numbers
> who do their task perfunctorily, as we say, or just
> to pass, and as badly as they dare, — there are the
> working-men, on whom the burden of the business
> falls, — those who love work, and love to see it
> rightly done, who finish their task for its own sake;
> and the state and the world is happy, that has the
> most of such finishers. The world will always do
> justice at last to such finishers: it cannot otherwise.
> He who has acquired the ability, may wait securely
> the occasion of making it felt and appreciated, and
> know that it will not loiter. Men talk as if victory were
> something fortunate. Work is victory. Wherever work
> is done, victory is obtained. There is no chance, and
> no blanks. You want but one verdict: if you have your
> own, you are secure of the rest.[2]

Work is victory. Yes, so long as we judge by effort. And yet we know that the world demands results—and we desire that our efforts will be effective.

Emerson thought that we ought not to be shocked when powerful people over-extend.

> We say that success is constitutional; depends on a
> plus condition of mind and body, on power of work,
> on courage; that it is of main efficacy in carrying

---

1   *Leaves of Grass*, A Song of Joy (WW)
2   *Conduct of Life*, Worship (RWE)

> on the world, and, though rarely found in the right
> state for an article of commerce, but oftener in the
> supersaturate or excess, which makes it dangerous
> and destructive, yet it cannot be spared, and must
> be had in that form, and absorbents provided to
> take off its edge.[1]

Most of us have mixed feelings about individuals whose business success takes them to a level of worldly power that we can barely imagine. We look on with a compound of envy, suspicion, resentment, and guarded admiration. I suppose that most of us would join Hafiz in approval of the entrepreneurial impulse.

> This affirmative force is in one, and is not in
> another, as one horse has the spring in him, and
> another in the whip. "On the neck of the young
> man," said Hafiz, " sparkles no gem so gracious as
> enterprise."[2]

In stories of persons rising to success, we prefer that they have struggled on the way up. It seems fitting that great prizes should be hard-won. About the proportioning of effort to reward, in *The Tempest,* Shakespeare has the protagonist-magician Prospero create a situation in which his daughter falls in love with a handsome prince, and he with her. Prospero feigns doubts about the prince, and puts him to trials as though to test his merit—but Prospero tells the audience the real reason for the trials is to increase the value, to the prince, of his daughter's love.

> They are both in either's powers;
> but this swift business I must uneasy make,
> lest too light winning
> Make the prize light.[3]

---

1   *Conduct of Life,* Power (RWE)
2   *Conduct of Life,* Power (RWE)
3   *The Tempest,* Act I, Scene 2 (WS)

What we gain through difficulty we rate higher than what comes to us easily and painlessly. Emerson wrote of the variety of needs that compose a person's motivation,

> All the functions of human duty irritate and lash him forward, bemoaning and chiding, until they are performed. He wants friends, employment, knowledge, power, house and land, wife and children, honor and fame; he has religious wants, aesthetic wants, domestic, civil, humane wants. One by one, day after day he learns to coin his wishes into facts. He has his calling, homestead, social connection, and personal power, and thus, at the end of fifty years, his soul is appeased by seeing some sort of correspondence between his wish and his possession.[1]

Success was fine with Emerson—he wanted it for himself. But he insisted on substance and understatement.

> Now, though I am by no means sure that the reader will assent to all my propositions, yet I think we shall agree in my first rule for success, — that we shall drop the brag and the advertisement, and take Michel Angelo's course, "to confide in one's self, and be something of worth and value."[2]

> Success, or a fortunate genius, seems to depend on a happy adjustment of heart and brain; on a due proportion, hard to hit, of moral and mental power.[3]

Individuals who think that they owe all their success to themselves are deluded.

> The Genius of our life is jealous of individuals, and will not have any individual great, except through the general. There is no choice to genius. A great man does not wake up on some fine morning, and say, I am full of life, I will go to sea, and find an

---

1   *Society and Solitude,* Old Age (RWE)
2   *Society and Solitude,* Success (RWE)
3   *Representative Men,* Swedenborg; or, the Mystic (RWE)

> Antarctic continent: to-day I will square the circle:
> I will ransack botany, and find a new food for man:
> I have a new architecture in my mind: I foresee a
> new mechanic power: no, but he finds himself in
> the river of the thoughts and events, forced onward
> by the ideas and necessities of his contemporaries.
> … Every master has found his materials collected,
> and his power lay in his sympathy with his people,
> and in his love of the materials he wrought in. What
> an economy of power! and what a compensation
> for the shortness of life! All is done to his hand.
> The world has brought him thus far on his way.
> The human race has gone out before him, sunk the
> hills, filled the hollows, and bridged the rivers. Men,
> nations, poets, artisans, women, all have worked
> for him, and he enters into their labors. Choose any
> other thing, out of the line of tendency, out of the
> national feeling and history, and he would have all
> to do for himself: his powers would be expended in
> the first preparations.[1]

The twentieth-century science historian Thomas Kuhn put it this way:

> The extent of innovation that any individual can
> produce is necessarily limited, for each individual
> must employ in his research the tools that he
> acquires from a traditional education, and he
> cannot in his own lifetime replace them all.[2]

Grace

We aspire to be gracious in our manner and graceful in our actions. Emerson thought that good manners were a key to success in every area of life.

> The power of manners is incessant, — an element
> as unconcealable as fire. The nobility cannot in any
> country be disguised, and no more in a republic

---

1 *Representative Men,* Shakespeare; or, the Poet (RWE)
2 *The Copernican Revolution: Planetary Astronomy in the Development of Western Thought,* Thomas S. Kuhn

or a democracy, than in a kingdom. No man can
resist their influence.[1]

This idea of a natural nobility came at a time when the
class consciousness of the British Empire lingered in American
air. In Emerson's framing, the category of ladies and gentlemen
was not completely defined by birth, wealth, or education—
those links were palpable but indirect, as they remain today.

Emerson believed that the fine points of social behavior
affect our lives more than we realize, and reach into every
corner of our relations with others.

> Your manners are always under examination, and
> by committees little suspected, — a police in
> citizens' clothes, — but are awarding or denying
> you very high prizes when you least think of it.
> We talk much of utilities, — but 'tis our manners
> that associate us. In hours of business, we go
> to him who knows, or has, or does this or that
> which we want, and we do not let our taste or
> feeling stand in the way. But this activity over, we
> return to the indolent state, and wish for those
> we can be at ease with; those who will go where
> we go, whose manners do not offend us, whose
> social tone chimes with ours. When we reflect
> on their persuasive and cheering force; how they
> recommend, prepare, and draw people together;
> how, in all clubs, manners make the members;
> how manners make the fortune of the ambitious
> youth; that, for the most part, his manners marry
> him, and, for the most part, he marries manners;
> when we think what keys they are, and to what
> secrets; what high lessons and inspiring tokens
> of character they convey; and what divination is
> required in us, for the reading of this fine telegraph,
> we see what range the subject has, and what
> relations to convenience, power, and beauty.[2]

---

1   *Conduct of Life,* Behavior (RWE)
2   *Representative Men,* Shakespeare; or, the Poet (RWE)

Among the several points above is the recognition of
the powers of "fine divination" that we use to evaluate one
another's social savvy. Brains keep busy with such work in all
vertebrates for whom smooth functioning of sociality is critical
to species survival.

Yankee that he was, Emerson advocated a low-key personal
style and preferred a polite social distance.

> Coolness and absence of heat and haste indicate
> fine qualities. A gentleman makes no noise: a lady
> is serene.[1]

> The mark of the man of the world is absence of
> pretension. He does not make a speech; he takes
> a low business-tone, avoids all brag, is nobody,
> dresses plainly, promises not at all, performs
> much, speaks in monosyllables, hugs his fact. He
> calls his employment by its lowest name, and so
> takes from evil tongues their sharpest weapon. His
> conversation clings to the weather and the news,
> yet he allows himself to be surprised into thought,
> and the unlocking of his learning and philosophy.[2]

> The complement of this graceful self-respect, and
> that of all the points of good breeding I most require
> and insist upon, is deference. I like that every chair
> should be a throne, and hold a king. I prefer a
> tendency to stateliness, to an excess of fellowship.
> Let the incommunicable objects of nature and
> the metaphysical isolation of man teach us
> independence. Let us not be too much acquainted.[3]

> People masquerade before us in their fortunes,
> titles, offices, and connections, as academic or
> civil presidents, or senators, or professors, or great
> lawyers, and impose on the frivolous, and a good
> deal on each other, by these fames. At least, it

---

1 *Essays: Second Series,* Manners (RWE)
2 *Conduct of Life,* Worship (RWE)
3 *Essays: Second Series,* Manners (RWE)

is a point of prudent good manners to treat these reputations tenderly, as if they were merited.[1]

I enjoy the humor in that last sentence—the ironic link of prudence to kindness.

The subtle skills required by the social graces are difficult to observe and to mark; they are nearly invisible; only their effect is felt. They cannot be conveyed by instruction.

> Who dare assume to guide a youth, a maid,
> to perfect manners? — the golden mean is so
> delicate, difficult, — say frankly, unattainable. What
> finest hands would not be clumsy to sketch the
> genial precepts of the young girl's demeanor? The
> chances seem infinite against success; and yet
> success is continually attained. There must not be
> secondariness, and 'tis a thousand to one that her
> air and manner will at once betray that she is not
> primary, but that there is some other one or many of
> her class, to whom she habitually postpones herself.
> But Nature lifts her easily, and without knowing it,
> over these impossibilities, and we are continually
> surprised with graces and felicities not only
> unteachable, but undescribable.[2]

When a writer characterizes something as "undescribable," the grace of humility is raised into view. Emerson was similarly humble about the grace of beauty. *Who can analyze the nameless charm?*

> Beauty is ever that divine thing the ancients
> esteemed it. It is, they said, the flowering of virtue.
> Who can analyze the nameless charm which
> glances from one and another face and form?
> We are touched with emotions of tenderness and
> complacency, but we cannot find whereat this dainty
> emotion, this wandering gleam point. It is destroyed
> for the imagination by any attempt to refer it to
> organization. Nor does it point to any relations of

---

1   *Conduct of Life,* Behavior (RWE)
2   *Conduct of Life,* Behavior (RWE)

friendship or love that society knows and has, but, as it seems to me, to a quite other and unattainable sphere, to relations of transcendant delicacy and sweetness, a true faerie land; to what roses and violets hint and foreshow. We cannot get at beauty. Its nature is like opaline doves'-neck lustres, hovering and evanescent.[1]

Shakespeare had Romeo put it this way:

But, soft! what light through yonder window breaks?
It is the east, and Juliet is the sun.
Arise, fair sun, and kill the envious moon,
Who is already sick and pale with grief,
That thou her maid art far more fair than she.
Two of the fairest stars in all the heaven,
Having some business, do entreat her eyes
To twinkle in their spheres till they return.
What if her eyes were there, they in her head?
The brightness of her cheek would shame those stars,
As daylight doth a lamp; her eyes in heaven
Would through the airy region stream so bright
That birds would sing and think it were not night.[2]

Emerson mentioned various kinds of beauty. We aspire to such beauties as can be cultivated.

Beauty is the form under which the intellect prefers to study the world. All privilege is that of beauty; for there are many beauties; as, of general nature, of the human face, and form, of manners, of brain, or method, moral beauty, or beauty of the soul.
I am warned by the ill fate of many philosophers not to attempt a definition of Beauty. I will rather enumerate a few of its qualities. We ascribe beauty to that which is simple; which has no superfluous parts; which exactly answers its end; which stands related to all things; which is the mean of many

---

1   *Essays,* Love (RWE)
2   *Romeo and Juliet,* Act II Scene 2 (WS)

extremes. It is the most enduring quality, and the most ascending quality.[1]

When his mood was upbeat, patient, and world-embracing, Emerson could find something to admire in every person.

> Every individual nature has its own beauty. One is struck in every company, at every fireside, with the riches of nature, when he hears so many new tones, all musical, sees in each person original manners, which have a proper and peculiar charm, and reads new expressions of face.[2]

The quantity of truth in this rests on the attitude of the observer. One is struck at other times with shallowness and absence of music. Emerson generally sought to emphasize the positive.

> Beauty is, even in the beautiful, occasional, — or, as one has said, culminating and perfect only a single moment, before which it is unripe, and after which it is on the wane. But beauty is never quite absent from our eyes. Every face, every figure, suggests its own right and sound estate.[3]

> But not less does Nature furnish us with every sign of grace and goodness. The delicious faces of children, the beauty of school-girls, "the sweet seriousness of sixteen," the lofty air of well-born, well-bred boys, the passionate histories in the looks and manners of youth and early manhood, and the varied power in all that well-known company that escort us through life, — we know how these forms thrill, paralyze, provoke, inspire, and enlarge us.[4]

For Emerson, the beauty of women was foremost.

---

1   *Conduct of Life,* Beauty (RWE)
2   *Society and Solitude,* Domestic Life (RWE)
3   *Society and Solitude,* Domestic Life (RWE)
4   *Conduct of Life,* Beauty (RWE)

> It costs a beautiful person no exertion to paint her
> image on our eyes; yet how splendid is that benefit![1]
>
> A beautiful woman is a practical poet, taming her
> savage mate, planting tenderness, hope, and
> eloquence, in all whom she approaches. Some
> favors of condition must go with it, since a certain
> serenity is essential, but we love its reproofe and
> superiorities. Nature wishes that woman should
> attract man, yet she often cunningly moulds into her
> face a little sarcasm, which seems to say, 'Yes, I am
> willing to attract, but to attract a little better kind of a
> man than any I yet behold.'[2]

That concluding line gleams with Emerson's wit. When he delivered it in a lecture, surely the audience laughed, and I'm guessing he paused to give them time to do so before he continued:

> We can pardon pride, when a woman possesses
> such a figure, that wherever she stands, or moves, or
> leaves a shadow on the wall, or sits for a portrait to
> the artist, she confers a favor on the world. And yet
> — it is not beauty that inspires the deepest passion.
> Beauty without grace, beauty without expression,
> tires.[3]

The image of the shadow on the wall suggests the ways confidence and self-trust lend grace.

> Let the maiden, with erect soul, walk serenely on
> her way, accept the hint of each new experience,
> try, in turn, all the gifts God offers her, that she may
> learn the power and the charm, that like a new dawn
> radiating out of the deep of space, her new-born
> being is. The fair girl, who repels interference by a
> decided and proud choice of influences, so careless
> of pleasing, so wilful and lofty, inspires every

---

1   *Representative Men,* Uses of Great Men (RWE)
2   *Conduct of Life,* Beauty (RWE)
3   *Conduct of Life,* Beauty (RWE)

beholder with somewhat of her own nobleness. The
silent heart encourages her; O friend, never strike
sail to a fear. Come into port greatly, or sail with
God the seas. Not in vain you live, for every passing
eye is cheered and refined by the vision.[1]

Living in the Present

To *accept the hint of each new experience,* we need to be paying
attention. We aspire to savor and linger in the present, but
we find it difficult to do—there's something in our nervous
systems that thwarts us.

> Man postpones or remembers; he does not live in
> the present, but with reverted eye laments the past,
> or, heedless of the riches that surround him, stands
> on tiptoe to foresee the future. He cannot be happy
> and strong until he too lives with nature in the
> present, above time.[2]

The success of our species stems from that impulse
to *stand on tiptoe to foresee the future* because, when prepared
for contingencies, our ancestors raised more children to
adulthood. This inherited anxiety leaves us challenged to exist
calm and satisfied in the present without some distraction or
entertainment. Between diversions we review the past or think
ahead. The future is uncertain; we want to be prepared for
whatever it might bring. What is the likelihood, with the minds
we have, that we can *live above time?* We have a decent chance,
though, to be present with our attention to companions.

> Let us be poised, and wise, and our own, today.
> Let us treat the men and women well: treat them
> as if they were real: perhaps they are. Men live in
> their fancy, like drunkards whose hands are too
> soft and tremulous for successful labor. It is a
> tempest of fancies, and the only ballast I know, is
> a respect to the present hour. Without any shadow
> of doubt, amidst this vertigo of shows and politics,

---

1   *Essays,* Heroism (RWE)
2   *Essays,* Self-Reliance (RWE)

> I settle myself ever the firmer in the creed, that we
> should not postpone and refer and wish, but do
> broad justice where we are, by whomsoever we
> deal with, accepting our actual companions and
> circumstances, however humble or odious, as the
> mystic officials to whom the universe has delegated
> its whole pleasure for us.[1]

What does *doing broad justice* look like? Giving others
the benefit of the doubt. Bringing cheer and sincerity to our
communications with strangers, acquaintances, friends, and
family members.

> I honor that man whose ambition it is, not to win
> laurels in the state or the army, not to be a jurist or
> a naturalist, not to be a poet or a commander, but
> to be a master of living well, and to administer the
> offices of master or servant, of husband, father, and
> friend. But it requires as much breadth of power
> for this as for those other functions, — as much, or
> more.[2]

Self-realization

Whatever direction our ambitions take us, whatever forms
of personal power we choose to cultivate, our fundamental goal
is self-realization—the process of becoming the best and fullest
of what is ours to become. Whitman was in an ecstasy on the
subject of his own self-realization.

> Have you reckon'd a thousand acres much? have
> you reckon'd the earth much?
>   Have you practis'd so long to learn to read?
>   Have you felt so proud to get at the meaning of
> poems?
>   Stop this day and night with me and you shall
> possess the origin of
>   all poems,

---

1 *Essays: Second Series,* Experience (RWE)
2 *Society and Solitude,* Domestic Life (RWE)

You shall possess the good of the earth and sun, (there are millions
    of suns left,)
  You shall no longer take things at second or third hand, nor look through
    the eyes of the dead, nor feed on the spectres in books,
  You shall not look through my eyes either, nor take things from me,
  You shall listen to all sides and filter them from your self.

Apart from the pulling and hauling stands what I am,
  Stands amused, complacent, compassionating, idle, unitary,
  Looks down, is erect, or bends an arm on an impalpable certain rest,
  Looking with side-curved head curious what will come next,
  Both in and out of the game and watching and wondering at it.
I am of old and young, of the foolish as much as the wise,
  Regardless of others, ever regardful of others,
  Maternal as well as paternal, a child as well as a man,
  Stuff'd with the stuff that is coarse and stuff'd with the stuff that is fine,

I resist any thing better than my own diversity,
  Breathe the air but leave plenty after me,
  And am not stuck up, and am in my place.
Do you guess I have some intricate purpose?
  Well I have, for the Fourth-month showers have, and the mica on the
    side of a rock has.
  Do you take it I would astonish?
  Does the daylight astonish? does the early redstart twittering through the woods?
  Do I astonish more than they?

I know I am solid and sound,
  To me the converging objects of the universe
perpetually flow,
  All are written to me, and I must get what the
writing means.[1]

The sympathy between the poet Whitman and the lecturer Emerson is strongest on this theme. Fourteen years before the first edition of *Leaves of Grass,* Emerson published the following:

> What a man does, that he has. What has he to do with hope or fear? In himself is his might. Let him regard no good as solid, but that which is in his nature, and which must grow out of him as long as he exists. The goods of fortune may come and go like summer leaves; let him play with them, and scatter them on every wind as the momentary signs of his infinite productiveness.
>
> He may have his own. A man's genius, the quality that differences him from every other, the susceptibility to one class of influences, the selection of what is fit for him, the rejection of what is unfit, determines for him the character of the universe. As a man thinketh, so is he, and as a man chooseth, so is he. [2]

This is the purest Emersonian doctrine, a family of themes that ran through his teaching from first to last.

> The basis of good manners is self-reliance. Necessity is the law of all who are not self-possessed. Those who are not self-possessed, obtrude, and pain us. Some men appear to feel that they belong to a Pariah caste. They fear to offend, they bend and apologize, and walk through life with a timid step. As we sometimes dream that we are in a well-dressed company without any coat, so Godfrey acts ever as if he suffered from some mortifying circumstance. The hero should find himself at home, wherever he is; should impart

---

1   *Leaves of Grass,* Song of Myself (WW)
2   *Essays,* Spiritual Laws (RWE)

comfort by his own security and good-nature to all
beholders. The hero is suffered to be himself.[1]

His validation of each person's individuality helps Emerson
hold his place on bookshelves.

> It seems as if the Deity dressed each soul which
> he sends into nature in certain virtues and powers
> not communicable to other men, and, sending
> it to perform one more turn through the circle of
> beings, wrote "Not transferable" and "Good for
> this trip only" on these garments of the soul. There
> is somewhat deceptive about the intercourse of
> minds. The boundaries are invisible, but they are
> never crossed. There is such good will to impart,
> and such good will to receive, that each threatens
> to become the other; but the law of individuality
> collects its secret strength: you are you, and I am I,
> and so we remain.[2]

The following is one of those places in which Emerson
describes his own situation and leaves it to us to determine
what value it has for ourselves. His life's work was as a writer
and speaker; he lets us know that sometimes he must proceed
as though what he had to say felt adequate to himself.

> A man can only speak, so long as he does not feel
> his speech to be partial and inadequate. It is partial,
> but he does not see it to be so, whilst he utters
> it. As soon as he is released from the instinctive
> and particular, and sees its partiality, he shuts his
> mouth in disgust. For, no man can write anything,
> who does not think that what he writes is for the
> time the history of the world; or do anything well,
> who does not esteem his work to be of importance.
> My work may be of none, but I must not think it
> of none, or I shall not do it with impunity. In like
> manner, there is throughout nature something
> mocking, something that leads us on and on, but

---

1   *Conduct of Life,* Behavior (RWE)
2   *Representative Men,* Uses of Great Men (RWE)

> arrives nowhere, keeps no faith with us. All promise
> outruns the performance.[1]

> No man can quite emancipate himself from his
> age and country, or produce a model in which the
> education, the religion, the politics, usages, and
> arts, of his times shall have no share. Though he
> were never so original, never so wilful and fantastic,
> he cannot wipe out of his work every trace of the
> thoughts amidst which it grew.[2]

This humility, the insight that we cannot escape our times and places, might limit our philosophical aspirations, but not our effort to live *good hours*.

> To finish the moment, to find the journey's end in
> every step of the road, to live the greatest number
> of good hours, is wisdom.[3]

A fine-sounding sentence! What does it mean? *To finish the moment* has to do with focus, attention, and mental follow-through. What makes an hour good? No one thing. Our quest for character involves learning what good hours are, for ourselves, and how we can cultivate a balance among our activities to make best use of our time. We try for *wisdom*; for a well thought out selection of goals and plans and actions.

> Wisdom is like electricity. There is no permanently
> wise man, but men capable of wisdom, who,
> being put into certain company, or other favorable
> conditions, become wise for a short time, as
> glasses rubbed acquire electric power for a while.[4]

The obstacles to self-realization are formidable.

> He is the considerer, the prudent, taking in sail,
> counting stock, husbanding his means, believing
> that a man has too many enemies, than that he can

---

1   *Essays: Second Series,* Nature (RWE)
2   *Essays,* Art (RWE)
3   *Essays: Second Series,* Experience (RWE)
4   *Society and Solitude,* Clubs (RWE)

afford to be his own; that we cannot give ourselves too many advantages, in this unequal conflict, with powers so vast and unweariable ranged on one side, and this little, conceited, vulnerable popinjay that a man is, bobbing up and down into every danger, on the other. It is a position taken up for better defence, as of more safety, and one that can be maintained; and it is one of more opportunity and range: as, when we build a house, the rule is, to set it not too high nor too low, under the wind, but out of the dirt.[1]

The considerer, the prudent. Confidence like Whitman's, "I know I am solid and sound, To me the converging objects of the universe perpetually flow," is not ours at every hour. Sailing ships stay afloat by taking in sail in stormy weather. Our voyage lasts through many days and weathers, and we must adjust to circumstances. Reaching the later part of life, we hope that we have learned something. Emerson offers this encouragement:

> When life has been well spent, age is a loss of what it can well spare, — muscular strength, organic instincts, gross bulk, and works that belong to these. But the central wisdom, which was old in infancy, is young in fourscore years, and, dropping off obstructions, leaves in happy subjects the mind purified and wise.[2]

> He who has cast off the common motives of humanity and has ventured to trust himself for a task-master— high be his heart, faithful his will, clear his sight, that he may in good earnest be doctrine, society, law to himself, that a simple purpose may be to him as strong as iron necessity is to others.[3]

High aspirations are fundamental to character. Circumstances have a bearing on their attainment.

---

1   *Representative Men,* Montaigne; or, the Skeptic (RWE)
2   *Society and Solitude,* Old Age (RWE)
3   *Essays,* Self-Reliance (RWE)

Circumstances

Temperament

The inner ring of circumstances is characteristics of our selves. The wish to control our own destiny tempts us to believe that we can change, under the direction of our will, the kind of person we are. One reason this is difficult is that we cannot view our own personality objectively.

> Temperament enters fully into the system of illusions, and shuts us in a prison of glass which we cannot see. There is an optical illusion about every person we meet. In truth, they are all creatures of given temperament, which will appear in a given character, whose boundaries they will never pass: but we look at them, they seem alive, and we presume there is impulse in them. In the moment, it seems impulse; in the year, in the lifetime, it turns out to be a certain uniform tune which the revolving barrel of the music-box must play. Men resist the conclusion in the morning, but adopt it as the evening wears on, that temper prevails over everything of time, place, and condition, and is inconsumable in the flames of religion.[1]

This is one of Emerson's busy paragraphs. It begins by characterizing our own temperaments as inescapable transparent bubbles, then switches to our perceptions of the people around us, asserting that each is permanently limited by temperament. Coming from an apostle of individualism, this is a pessimistic view. A music box is limited to a single tune. A more moderate trope would have been to compare temperament to a given instrument, say, a clarinet, that can never stop being a clarinet but has nonetheless a considerable range of tones and tunes, and can be played better or worse.

The citation above concludes that no external circumstance, including religion, can overcome what we are at our core. We

---

1   *Essays: Second Series,* Experience (RWE)

can accept this, if we interpret it to mean that this inner ring of circumstance will remain with us through our transitions and growth. And yet,

> No change of circumstances can repair a defect of character. ... I am always environed by myself.[1]

> Wise men read very sharply all your private history in your look and gait and behavior. The whole economy of nature is bent on expression. ... The face and eyes reveal what the spirit is doing, how old it is, what aims it has. The eyes indicate the antiquity of the soul, or, through how many forms it has already ascended.[2]

Do we wear our character in ways legible to those paying attention? In Shakespeare's *The Tempest,* a teenaged girl named Miranda has been raised by her father on a desert island. The wizard-like father causes a prince to be shipwrecked and, by magic, transported ashore. The young man's good looks leave Miranda weak-kneed. When her father argues that she cannot yet know the fellow's quality, she argues that:

> There's nothing ill can dwell in such a temple:
> If the ill spirit have so fair a house,
> Good things will strive to dwell with't.[3]

Miranda expects only the best from such a handsome young man. She is naïve, having had no prior social experience. But when I ask groups whether the three lines above capture a strong human tendency, I see many nods.

In *Richard III*, Shakespeare goes the opposite direction, using deformity as an emblem of villainy. In the opening speech of the play Richard declares his envy, his resentment, and his evil intentions.

---

1   *Essays: Second Series,* Character (RWE)
2   *Conduct of Life,* Behavior (RWE)
3   *The Tempest,* Act I, Scene 2 (WS)

But I, that am not shaped for sportive tricks,
Nor made to court an amorous looking-glass;
I, that am rudely stamp'd, and want love's majesty
To strut before a wanton ambling nymph;
I, that am curtail'd of this fair proportion,
Cheated of feature by dissembling nature,
Deformed, unfinish'd, sent before my time
Into this breathing world, scarce half made up,
And that so lamely and unfashionable
That dogs bark at me as I halt by them;
Why, I, in this weak piping time of peace,
Have no delight to pass away the time,
Unless to spy my shadow in the sun
And descant on mine own deformity:
And therefore, since I cannot prove a lover,
To entertain these fair well-spoken days,
I am determined to prove a villain
And hate the idle pleasures of these days.
Plots have I laid, inductions dangerous,
By drunken prophecies, libels and dreams,
To set my brother Clarence and the king
In deadly hate the one against the other:
And if King Edward be as true and just
As I am subtle, false and treacherous...
Dive, thoughts, down to my soul...[1]

Shakespeare made his Richard a thoroughly despicable character. We learn from early age to look for "bad guys" and "good guys" in stories, and come to realize that they are images for impulses we all have in which our selfish interests duel with our better intentions. Emerson wrote of the way certain leanings tend to run in families:

How shall a man escape from his ancestors, or
draw off from his veins the black drop which he
drew from his father's or his mother's life? It often
appears in a family, as if all the qualities of the

---

1   *Richard III*, Act 1 Scene 1 (WS)

> progenitors were potted in several jars, — some
> ruling quality in each son or daughter of the house,
> — and sometimes the unmixed temperament, the
> rank unmitigated elixir, the family vice, is drawn
> off in a separate individual, and the others are
> proportionally relieved. We sometimes see a change
> of expression in our companion, and say, his father,
> or his mother, comes to the windows of his eyes,
> and sometimes a remote relative. In different hours,
> a man represents each of several of his ancestors,
> as if there were seven or eight of us rolled up in
> each man's skin, — seven or eight ancestors at
> least, — and they constitute the variety of notes for
> that new piece of music which his life is.
> Men are what their mothers made them.[1]

Emerson joins genes and upbringing with the statement "Men are what their mothers made them."

> Manners are partly factitious, but, mainly, there
> must be capacity for culture in the blood. Else all
> culture is vain. The obstinate prejudice in favor
> of blood, which lies at the base of the feudal and
> monarchical fabrics of the old world, has some
> reason in common experience.[2]

The obstinate prejudice in favor of blood, like any prejudice, discomforts fair-minded persons. When the question of whether a person's qualities stem from nature (their genes) or nurture (their upbringing) arises, we want to advocate for the dominance of nurture because not doing so opens an intellectual door for the major *isms*: racism and sexism—the prejudices we abhor. Around 1970 we hypothesized that girls and boys were shaped and limited in important ways if we gave trucks to one gender and dolls to the other. But as that generation passed through the years of parenthood, experience taught otherwise. Happily, it became clear that wearing pink and playing with Barbies as girls does not prevent women from

---

1   *Conduct of Life,* Fate (RWE)
2   *Conduct of Life,* Behavior (RWE)

loving science or seeking political power. Nor, we have seen, does dark skin prevent individuals from have brilliant insights and/or being elected President of the United States. Meanwhile, studies of identical twins separated at birth convincingly show the importance of our genes in determining who we are: adult twins raised in different households exhibit dramatic similarities.

Gender

As our society has grown more tolerant of individual differences and more accepting of behavior previously derided as abnormal, most of us have become more flexible in our expectations regarding gender and sexual orientation. That said, gender, one way or another, is part of that ring of circumstances within which we must dwell throughout our lives.

Margaret Fuller wrote long before women were allowed to vote. Her book, *Woman in the Nineteenth Century,* was an argument for equal rights. It included this passage.

> Male and female represent the two sides of
> the great radical dualism. But, in fact, they are
> perpetually passing into one another. Fluid hardens
> to solid, solid rushes to fluid. There is no wholly
> masculine man, no purely feminine woman.

Radical is used here in the sense of "fundamental." Fuller makes the point, ahead of her time, that although physical production of eggs and sperm is dual, gender-related attitudes and abilities are not; they are on a spectrum that maps imprecisely on physical traits.

> Sight must be verified by light before it can deserve
> the honors of piety and genius. Yet sight comes
> first, and of this sight of the world of causes, this
> approximation to the region of primitive motions,
> women I hold to be especially capable. Even
> without equal freedom with the other sex, they have
> already shown themselves so; and should these
> faculties have free play, I believe they will open new,

deeper and purer sources of joyous inspiration than
have as yet refreshed the earth.[1]

Fuller saw that men and women could not progress
separately.

> By Man I mean both man and woman; these are
> the two halves of one thought. I lay no especial
> stress on the welfare of either. I believe that the
> development of the one cannot be effected without
> that of the other. My highest wish is that this truth
> should be distinctly and rationally apprehended,
> and the condition of life and freedom recognized
> as the same for the daughter and the sons of time;
> twin exponents of a divine thought.
>
> We would have every arbitrary barrier thrown down.
> We would have every path laid open to Woman
> as freely as to Man. Were this done, and a slight
> temporary fermentation allowed to subside, we
> should see crystallizations more pure and of more
> various beauty. We believe the divine energy would
> pervade nature to a degree unknown in the history
> of former ages, and that no discordant collision, but
> a ravishing harmony of the spheres, would ensue.[2]

Influenced by Fuller, Emerson and his circle began to call
for change in the status of women. Emerson made feminist-
sounding remarks but he had his own way of gently tempering
his stances.

> I esteem it a chief felicity of this country,
> that it excels in women. A certain awkward
> consciousness of inferiority in the men, may give
> rise to the new chivalry in behalf of Woman's
> Rights. Certainly, let her be as much better placed
> in the laws and in social forms, as the most zealous
> reformer can ask, but I confide so entirely in her
> inspiring and musical nature, that I believe only
> herself can show us how she shall be served.[3]

---

1   Margaret Fuller, *Woman in the Nineteenth Century*
2   Margaret Fuller, *Woman in the Nineteenth Century*
3   *Essays: Second Series*, Manners (RWE)

> In every company, there is not only the active
> and passive sex, but, in both men and women, a
> deeper and more important sex of mind, namely,
> the inventive or creative class of both men and
> women, and the uninventive or accepting class.[1]

Emerson was a gradualist.

> I suppose, the Parisian milliner who dresses the
> world from her imperious boudoir will know how
> to reconcile the Bloomer costume to the eye of
> mankind, and make it triumphant over Punch
> himself, by interposing the just gradations. I need
> not say, how wide the same law ranges; and how
> much it can be hoped to effect. All that is a little
> harshly claimed by progressive parties, may easily
> come to be conceded without question, if this
> rule be observed. Thus the circumstances may be
> easily imagined, in which woman may speak, vote,
> argue causes, legislate, and drive a coach, and
> all the most naturally in the world, if only it come
> by degrees. To this streaming or flowing belongs
> the beauty that all circular movement has; as, the
> circulation of waters, the circulation of the blood,
> the periodical motion of planets, the annual wave
> of vegetation, the action and reaction of Nature:
> and, if we follow it out, this demand in our thought
> for an ever-onward action, is the argument for the
> immortality.[2]

In some of his poems, Whitman rejected sexism.

> I am the poet of the woman the same as the man,
>   And I say it is as great to be a woman as to be a
> man,
>   And I say there is nothing greater than the mother
> of men.[3]

---

1   *Conduct of Life,* Power (RWE)
2   *Conduct of Life,* Beauty (RWE)
3   *Leaves of Grass,* Song of Myself (WW)

Whitman awarded women primacy as the sources of creativity, strength, and the ethics of fairness (justice) and kindness (sympathy).

> Unfolded only out of the inimitable poems of
> woman can come the
>   poems of man, (only thence have my poems
> come;)
>   Unfolded out of the strong and arrogant woman I
> love, only thence
>   can appear the strong and arrogant man I love,
>   Unfolded by brawny embraces from the well-
> muscled woman
>   love, only thence come the brawny embraces
> of the man,
>   Unfolded out of the folds of the woman's brain
> come all the folds
>   of the man's brain, duly obedient,
>   Unfolded out of the justice of the woman all
> justice is unfolded,
>   Unfolded out of the sympathy of the woman is all
> sympathy.[1]

Shakespeare's work is rich in commentary about gender. He made a feminist statement in *The Tempest,* when he had Miranda say to her beloved,

> **Miranda.** If you'll sit down,
> I'll bear your logs the while: pray, give me that;
> I'll carry it to the pile.
> **Ferdinand.** No, precious creature;
> I had rather crack my sinews, break my back,
> Than you should such dishonour undergo,
> While I sit lazy by.

---

1   *Leaves of Grass,* Unfolded out of the Folds (WW)

> **Miranda.** It would become me
> As well as it does you.[1]

As You Like It includes this dialogue between best girlfriends, who love Touchstone the clown but also like to tease him.

> **Celia.** Let us sit and mock the good housewife Fortune from her wheel, that her gifts may henceforth be bestowed equally.
> **Rosalind.** I would we could do so; for her benefits are mightily misplaced; and the bountiful blind woman doth most mistake in her gifts to women.
> **Celia.** 'Tis true; for those that she makes fair she scarce makes honest; and those that she makes honest she makes very ill-favouredly.
> **Rosalind**. Nay; now thou goest from Fortune's office to Nature's:
> Fortune reigns in gifts of the world, not in the lineaments of Nature.
> *Enter Touchstone*
> **Celia.** No; when Nature hath made a fair creature, may she not by Fortune fall into the fire? Though Nature hath given us wit to flout at Fortune, hath not Fortune sent in this fool to cut off the argument?
> **Rosalind.** Indeed, there is Fortune too hard for Nature, when Fortune makes Nature's natural the cutter-off of Nature's wit.
> **Celia.** Peradventure this is not Fortune's work neither, but Nature's, who perceiveth our natural wits too dull to reason of such goddesses, and hath sent this natural for our whetstone; for always the dullness of the fool is the whetstone of the wits. How now, wit! Whither wander you?[2]

Fate

Rosalind and Celia's dialogues are intended to amuse rather than to instruct. They mix gender-related quips with the

---

1   *The Tempest,* Act III, Scene 1 (WS)
2   *As You Like It,* Act I, Scene 2 (WS)

remarks about fate, a great circumstance that meets each of us at different levels every day—whether we are drawing cards in a game with children or receiving test results about a serious illness. The realm is that of luck, or fate, or chance. We employ those words and others when we speak of it, each having a slightly different sense. Most people can point to aspects of their lives that make them feel fortunate and to other aspects that feel unlucky.

Science has revealed much about cause and effect without diminishing the role of unanswerable chance. Shakespeare knew nothing of DNA when he wrote:

> It is the stars,
> The stars above us, govern our conditions;
> Else one self mate and mate could not beget
> Such different issues.[1]

Fate was sometimes placed in the control of *the stars*–at an unreachable distance. Other times those levers were put in the hands of divinities:

> As flies to wanton boys are we to th' gods.
> They kill us for their sport.[2]

> What can be avoided
> Whose end is purposed by the mighty gods?[3]

Remarkably little has changed over the 400 years between Shakespeare and us with respect to the encounter of human consciousness with chance. Philosophers still argue whether we can make actual choices or are only puppets in the hands of a predetermined order. Modern physics has found that very small things — molecules, atoms — act according to Heisenberg's uncertainty principle, and their location cannot be pinned down precisely. Some philosophers have cited

---

1   *King Lear*, Act IV, Scene 3 (WS)
2   *King Lear*, Act IV, Scene 1 (WS)
3   *Julius Caesar*, Act II, Scene 2 (WS)

this against determinism. The principle seems to support the intuitive perception that random events can trump our intentions, plans, and wishes. We cross our fingers in the hope that fortune will look kindly upon us.

> Fortune, good night; smile once more, turn thy wheel.[1]

Emily Dickinson wrote of fate:

> The Future never spoke –
> Nor will he like the Dumb
> Reveal by sign a Syllable
> Of his profound To Come-
>
> But when the News be ripe
> Presents it in the act –
> Forestalling Preparation –
> Escape – or Substitute –
>
> Indifferent to him
> The Dower[2] – as the Doom –
> His Office but to execute
> Fate's Telegram – to Him -[3]

Some individuals seem to have more than their share of bad luck, or of good.

> Be it art or hap,
> He hath spoken true: the very dice obey him;
> And in our sports my better cunning faints
> Under his chance.[4]

Here lies a basic unfairness in life. Fate sometimes deals catastrophes that make survivors permanent victims. Suffering

---

1 *King Lear*, Act II, Scene 2 (WS)
2 In this context, "dower" means the positive benefit, in contrast to "doom," the negative. Dower meant a widow's share of her husband's estate.
3 *The Future Never Spoke* , Emily Dickinson
4 *Antony and Cleopatra*, Act II, Scene 3 (WS)

and anger pervade their emotions and fence off every joy.
In literature, this lot is cast on Hamlet. His father, the good
king, died suddenly, succeeded to the throne by his brother,
Hamlet's uncle. Hamlet's mother soon marries the new king.
While Hamlet grieves all this misfortune, he learns that his
mother had been unfaithful and that his uncle had poisoned
the good king to take both crown and queen. These are
"The slings and arrows of outrageous fortune," that Hamlet
famously laments. The impact of this infuriating circumstance,
this dreadful fate, clouds Hamlet's judgment and results
in his killing others and meeting his own early death. In
Roman mythology, luck was deified as the goddess Fortuna,
symbolized by a wheel. These lines express Hamlet's rage at
fate.

> Out, out, thou strumpet Fortune!
> All you gods,
> In general synod take away her power;
> Break all the spokes and fellies[1] from her wheel,
> And bowl the round nave down the hill of heaven,[2]

Earlier in the same scene the feminization of fortune
provides bawdy comic relief.

> **Guildenstern.** Happy in that we are not over-
> happy.
> On Fortune's cap we are not the very button.
> **Hamlet.** Nor the soles of her shoe?
> **Rosencrantz.** Neither, my lord.
> **Hamlet.** Then you live about her waist, or in the
> middle of her favours?
> **Guildenstern.** Faith, her privates we.
> **Hamlet.** In the secret parts of Fortune? O! most
> true! she is a strumpet.[3]

Emerson acknowledged the role of chance in our lives.

---

1   "Fellies" are sections of a wheel's rim; the "nave" is the hub.
2   *Hamlet,* Act II, Scene 2 (WS)
3   *Hamlet,* Act II, Scene 2 (WS)

The results of life are uncalculated and uncalculable.[1]

Although in his first book he had characterized Nature as beneficent, Emerson came to see it as a source of danger as well as beauty.

The word Fate, or Destiny, expresses the sense of mankind, in all ages, — that the laws of the world do not always befriend, but often hurt and crush us. Fate, in the shape of Kinde or nature, grows over us like grass. We paint Time with a scythe; Love and Fortune, blind; and Destiny, deaf. We have too little power of resistance against this ferocity which champs us up. What front can we make against these unavoidable, victorious, maleficent forces?[2]

The planet is liable to shocks from comets, perturbations from planets, rendings from earth-quake and volcano, alterations of climate, precessions of equinoxes. …Providence has a wild, rough, incalculable road to its end, and it is of no use to try to whitewash its huge, mixed instrumentalities, or to dress up that terrific benefactor in a clean shirt and white neckcloth of a student in divinity.[3]

The element running through entire nature, which we popularly call Fate, is known to us as limitation. Whatever limits us, we call Fate.

When the gods in the Norse heaven were unable to bind the Fenris Wolf with steel or with weight of mountains, — the one he snapped and the other he spurned with his heel, — they put round his foot a limp band softer than silk or cobweb, and this held him: the more he spurned it, the stiffer it drew. So soft and so stanch is the ring of Fate.[4]

---

1   *Essays: Second Series,* Experience (RWE)
2   *Representative Men,* Montaigne; or, the Skeptic (RWE)
3   *Conduct of Life,* Fate (RWE)
4   *Conduct of Life,* Fate (RWE)

But Emerson went on to acknowledge and salute the strength of human resistance.

> Though Fate is immense, so is power, which
> is the other fact in the dual world, immense. If
> Fate follows and limits power, power attends
> and antagonizes Fate. We must respect Fate as
> natural history, but there is more than natural
> history. For who and what is this criticism that
> pries into the matter? Man is not order of nature,
> sack and sack, belly and members, link in a chain,
> nor any ignominious baggage, but a stupendous
> antagonism, a dragging together of the poles of
> the Universe. He betrays his relation to what is
> below him, — thick-skulled, small-brained, fishy,
> quadrumanous,[1] — quadruped ill-disguised, hardly
> escaped into biped, and has paid for the new
> powers by loss of some of the old ones. But the
> lightning which explodes and fashions planets,
> maker of planets and suns, is in him.[2]

Emerson attributes to humans the *lightning which explodes and fashions planets*—as though he foresaw the future human ability to release fusion energy. Human beings combat fate with science and technology. Any cardiac or cancer patient knows what that looks like in their own lives.

We notice circumstances that we don't like more often than those that are comfortable. Shakespeare gives an unhappy young woman this lament:

> O, how full of briers is this working-day world![3]

Some circumstances alter our perspective. Losing accustomed amenities can leave you appreciative of poorer comforts. This happens to King Lear.

---

1 "Quadrumanous" means using arms and legs for walking, like a chimpanzee
2 *Conduct of Life*, Fate (RWE)
3 *As You Like It*, Act I, Scene 3 (WS)

> I am cold. Where is this straw, my fellow?
> The art of our necessities is strange,
> That can make vile things precious.[1]

The ability to shift attitudes and adapt to challenges is celebrated by our writers.

> Adversity is the prosperity of the great. The faithful student learns the greatness of humility. He shall work in the dark, work against failure, pain, and ill-will. If he is insulted, he can be insulted; all his affair is not to insult.[2]

Who is Emerson's "faithful student"? Himself, for one, and others determined to learn their way through life. Emerson would have us try to avoid ill will—but staunchly stand our ground.

> Nature has made up her mind that what cannot defend itself shall not be defended.[3]

This remark should be kept in mind in the context of relationships. A seasoned therapist observed, "People don't like you better because you let them mistreat you."

Life's Seasons

Childhood and adolescence have many cares and concerns, plus a sense of growth, and hope for the future. Emerson loved children, watched them and thought about them.

> The child with his sweet pranks, the fool of his senses, commanded by every sight and sound, without any power to compare and rank his sensations, abandoned to a whistle or a painted chip, to a lead dragoon, or a ginger-bread-dog, individualizing everything, generalizing nothing, delighted with every new thing, lies down at night overpowered by the fatigue, which this day of

---

1 *King Lear,* Act III, Scene 2 (WS)
2 *Conduct of Life,* Worship (RWE)
3 *Society and Solitude,* Courage (RWE)

> continual pretty madness has incurred. But Nature
> has answered her purpose with the curly, dimpled
> lunatic. She has tasked every faculty, and has
> secured the symmetrical growth of the bodily
> frame, by all these attitudes and exertions, — an
> end of the first importance, which could not be
> trusted to any care less perfect than her own.[1]

> We are as ungrateful as children.[2]

As parent birds labor to feed their babies, their nestlings respond with urgent demands for more. They are instinctively entitled, keenly aware that life and the world are owed to them. And yet,

> 'Tis little we can do for each other. We accompany
> the youth with sympathy, and manifold old sayings
> of the wise, to the gate of the arena, but 'tis certain
> that not by strength of ours, or of the old sayings,
> but only on strength of his own, unknown to us
> or to any, he must stand or fall. … What we have,
> therefore, to say of life, is rather description, or, if
> you please, celebration, than available rules.[3]

Aspirations are apt to conflict with each other. Feelings and duties for family can cause strands of self-development to be deferred and virtuous determinations to be forgone. Madame de Staël concluded,

> No matter how resolute we are about our own
> conduct when it is based on sincere convictions,
> when others begin to suffer because of us, it is
> almost impossible not to reproach ourselves.[4]

Such conflicts arise in adulthood, when we shoulder responsibility for the well-being of others. Of this central phase of life, Margaret Fuller wrote,

---

1 *Essays: Second Series,* Nature (RWE)
2 *Essays: Second Series,* Nominalist and Realist (RWE)
3 *Conduct of Life,* Considerations by the Way (RWE)
4 *Ten Years of Exile,* Madame de Staël

I stand in the sunny noon of life. Objects no longer
glitter in the dews of morning, neither are yet
softened by the shadows of evening. Every spot is
seen, every chasm revealed. Climbing the dusty hill,
some fair effigies that once stood for symbols of
human destiny have been broken; those I still have
with me show defects in this broad light. Yet enough
is left, even by experience, to point distinctly to the
glories of that destiny; faint, but not to be mistaken
streaks of the future day. I can say with the bard,
> "Though many have suffered shipwreck,
> still beat noble hearts."
Always the soul says to us all, Cherish your best
hopes as a faith, and abide by them in action.[1]

Of the seasons of life, advancing age is a potent
circumstance. Fuller continued,

> It is time, indeed, that men and women both should
> cease to grow old in any other way than as the tree
> does, full of grace and honor. The hair of the artist
> turns white, but his eye shines clearer than ever, and
> we feel that age brings him maturity, not decay.

In his first collection of essays, Emerson offered
prescriptions for the aging, and complained about his elders.

> Nature abhors the old, and old age seems the only
> disease: all others run into this one. ... We grizzle
> every day; I see no need of it. Whilst we converse
> with what is above us, we do not grow old, but grow
> young.
>
> Infancy, youth, receptive, aspiring, with religious eye
> looking upward, counts itself nothing, and abandons
> itself to the instruction flowing from all sides. But
> the man and woman of seventy, assume to know all;
> throw up their hope; renounce aspiration; accept the
> actual for the necessary; and talk down to the young.
> Let them then become organs of the Holy Ghost; let

---

1   *Woman in the Nineteenth Century,* Margaret Fuller

> them be lovers; let them behold truth; and their eyes are uplifted, their wrinkles smoothed, they are perfumed again with hope and power. [1]

Renouncing aspiration and *accepting the actual for the necessary* describe a lack of traction for inner growth. What has that to do with aging? In the last sentence Emerson admits as much: *perfumed again with hope and power*. As for *talking down to the young*, this aging person feels talked down to by Emerson's paragraph. But as the Sage of Concord himself added years, his emphasis shifted.

> If, on a winter day, you should stand within a bell-glass, the face and color of the noon clouds would not indicate whether it were June or January; and if we did not find the reflection of ourselves in the eyes of the young people we could not know that the century-clock had seventy instead of twenty. How many men habitually believe that each chance passenger with whom they converse is of their own age, and presently find it was his father, and not his brother, whom they knew. [2]

> As men get on in life, they acquire a love for sincerity, and somewhat less solicitude to be lulled or amused. In the progress of the character, there is an increasing faith in the moral sentiment, and a decreasing faith in propositions. Young people admire talents, and particular excellences. As we grow older, we value total powers and effects, as the spirit, or quality of the man. We have another sight, and a new standard; an insight which disregards what is done for the eye, and pierces to the doer; an ear which hears not what men say, but hears what they do not say. [3]

---

1   *Essays,* Circles (RWE)
2   *Society and Solitude,* Old Age (RWE)
3   *Conduct of Life,* Worship (RWE)

Mortality

Of the circumstance of the mortality of ourselves and those we love, Emerson wrote,

> The lot of humanity is on these children. Danger, sorrow, and pain arrive to them, as to all.[1]

> Nature is no sentimentalist, — does not cosset or pamper us. We must see that the world is rough and surly, and will not mind drowning a man or a woman; but swallows your ship like a grain of dust. The cold, inconsiderate of persons, tingles your blood, benumbs your feet, freezes a man like an apple. The diseases, the elements, fortune, gravity, lightning, respect no persons. The way of Providence is a little rude. The habit of snake and spider, the snap of the tiger and other leapers and bloody jumpers, the crackle of the bones of his prey in the coil of the anaconda, — these are in the system, and our habits are like theirs.[2]

Swallows your ship like a grain of dust; freezes a man like an apple. Vigorous language with reference to the impartiality of fate and the violence of predation, with which in the closing line he identifies human beings—the apex predators on our planet. Emerson's inclusion of people in the system of nature calls up those core motivations—basic animal self-preservation, the drive to fulfill basic needs, for which available resources are recruited without reference to kindness or fairness. *Our habits are like theirs.*

Although twenty-first century American grown-ups fear death by tooth and claw only when we swim in the sea or hike in grizzly country, the nighttime fears of children show our primeval dreads. I recall a rocking chair in my childhood bedroom that became a bear when the lights went out. The fundamental motive to continue living drives us to avoid death, the apprehension of which haunts our imaginations.

---

1   *Essays,* Love (RWE)
2   *Conduct of Life,* Fate (RWE)

Every man beholds his human condition with a
degree of melancholy. As a ship aground is battered
by the waves, so man, imprisoned in mortal life, lies
open to the mercy of coming events.[1]

Although we think of Whitman cheerfully embracing all
that the world has to offer, *Leaves of Grass* often reminds us of
his exposure to suffering and death. During the Civil War, he
served the Union Army as a nurse.

Yea, Death, we bow our faces, veil our eyes to thee,
  We mourn the old, the young untimely drawn to
thee,
  The fair, the strong, the good, the capable,
  The household wreck'd, the husband and the wife,
the engulfed forger in his forge,
  The corpses in the whelming waters and the mud,
  The gather'd thousands to their funeral mounds,
and thousands never
    found or gather'd.

Then after burying, mourning the dead,
  (Faithful to them found or unfound, forgetting not,
bearing the
    past, here new musing,)
  A day—a passing moment or an hour—America
itself bends low,
  Silent, resign'd, submissive.

For I too have forgotten,
  (Wrapt in these little potencies of progress,
politics, culture,
    wealth, inventions, civilization,)
  Have lost my recognition of your silent ever-
swaying power, ye
    mighty, elemental throes,
  In which and upon which we float, and every one
of us is buoy'd.[2]

---

1   *Essays*, Intellect (RWE)
2   *Leaves of Grass*, A Voice from Death (WW)

Emerson's "imprisoned in mortal life" is echoed by Whitman's "bitter hug of mortality."

> And I say to mankind, Be not curious about God,
>   For I who am curious about each am not curious about God,
>   (No array of terms can say how much I am at peace about God and
>   about death.)
>
> And as to you Death, and you bitter hug of mortality, it is idle to
>   try to alarm me.[1]

After acknowledging the *bitter hug of mortality*, Whitman denies, with his usual brass, dreading life's end. Shakespeare's manly Roman heroes also derided the fear of death.

> Cowards die many times before their deaths;
> The valiant never taste of death but once.
> Of all the wonders that I yet have heard.
> It seems to me most strange that men should fear;
> Seeing that death, a necessary end,
> Will come when it will come.[2]

> **Brutus.** Fates, we will know your pleasures:
> That we shall die, we know; 'tis but the time
> And drawing days out, that men stand upon.
> **Cassius.** Why, he that cuts off twenty years of life
> Cuts off so many years of fearing death.[3]

Shakespeare's introspective Danish protagonist, Hamlet, who longs for death's release from psychological pain, chooses to defer death because of its unknowable sequel.

> For who would bear the whips and scorns of time,
> Th' oppressor's wrong, the proud man's contumely,
> The pangs of despis'd love, the law's delay,

---

1   *Leaves of Grass,* Song of Myself (WW)
2   *Julius Caesar,* Act II, Scene 2 (WS)
3   *Julius Caesar,* Act III, Scene 1 (WS)

> The insolence of office, and the spurns
> That patient merit of th' unworthy takes,
> When he himself might his quietus make
> With a bare bodkin? Who would these fardels[1] bear,
> To grunt and sweat under a weary life,
> But that the dread of something after death-
> The undiscover'd country, from whose bourn
> No traveller returns- puzzles the will,
> And makes us rather bear those ills we have
> Than fly to others that we know not of.[2]

When this theme was repeated by Emerson, he took it one hopeful step farther.

> The secret of heaven is kept from age to age. No imprudent, no sociable angel ever dropt an early syllable to answer the longings of saints, the fears of mortals. We should have listened on our knees to any favorite, who, by stricter obedience, had brought his thoughts into parallelism with the celestial currents, and could hint to human ears the scenery and circumstance of the newly parted soul. But it is certain that it must tally with what is best in nature. It must not be inferior in tone to the already known works of the artist who sculptures the globes of the firmament, and writes the moral law. It must be fresher than rainbows, stabler than mountains, agreeing with flowers, with tides, and the rising and setting of autumnal stars.[3]

The circumstance of the newly parted soul. Emerson always had one foot in the pulpit and the other in the circle of intellectuals who were his peers. The last half of the foregoing paragraph has words of comfort, a pastoral image that seems to accept the notion of the soul as each individual's ongoing effervescence. There he wrote as a minister, declining to declare that death means for human beings what it means for all organisms—

---

1   "Fardels" means burdens
2   *Hamlet*, Act III, Scene 1 (WS)
3   *Representative Men,* Swedenborg; or, the Mystic (RWE)

dissolution. Human consciousness wants to dress individual demise with fanciful imagery. For his intellectual, scientific, readers Emerson composed word music in a different key.

> The knowledge that we traverse the whole scale
> of being, from the centre to the poles of nature,
> and have some stake in every possibility, lends
> that sublime lustre to death, which philosophy and
> religion have too outwardly and literally striven to
> express in the popular doctrine of the immortality of
> the soul. The reality is more excellent than the report.
> Here is no ruin, no discontinuity, no spent ball. The
> divine circulations never rest nor linger. Nature is
> the incarnation of a thought, and turns to a thought
> again, as ice becomes water and gas. The world is
> mind precipitated, and the volatile essence is forever
> escaping again into the state of free thought.[1]

The world is mind precipitated. Because we don't know what preceded the Big Bang, nor why the universe exists, the first cause is as mysterious as ever. The human mind—why not compare its miraculous capabilities to the unknown origin of matter and energy? Why not, if we wish, call them both *divine circulations* and imagine that our minds evaporate into eternal existence?

> All that respects the individual is temporary and
> prospective, like the individual himself, who is
> ascending out of his limits, into a catholic existence.[2]

> If there is a wish for immortality, and no evidence,
> why not say just that?[3]

I admire the pithy flatness of this rhetorical question. It leads to an accepting, resigned, attitude toward death. In *Antony and Cleopatra,* when circumstances doomed the queen, her insightful companion put it this way:

---

1   *Essays: Second Series,* Nature (RWE)
2   *Representative Men,* Uses of Great Men (RWE)
3   *Representative Men,* Montaigne; or, the Skeptic (RWE)

> Finish, good lady; the bright day is done,
> And we are for the dark.[1]

Virginia Woolf has the heroine of *To the Lighthouse* reflect:

> ...the monotonous fall of the waves on the beach,
> which for the most part beat a measured and
> soothing tattoo to her thoughts and seemed
> consolingly to repeat over and over again as she
> sat with the children the words of some old cradle
> song, murmured by nature, "I am guarding you—I
> am your support," but at other times suddenly
> and unexpectedly, especially when her mind
> raised itself slightly from the task actually in hand,
> had no such kindly meaning, but like a ghostly
> roll of drums remorselessly beat the measure
> of life, made one think of the destruction of the
> island and its engulfment in the sea, and warned
> her whose day had slipped past in one quick
> doing after another that it was all ephemeral as a
> rainbow—this sound which had been obscured
> and concealed under the other sounds suddenly
> thundered hollow in her ears and made her look up
> with an impulse of terror.[2]

One of Emerson's relatives by marriage was another Concord resident, Sarah Bradford Ripley, whose linguistic and scientific achievements, and her ability to tutor teetering Harvard students, put her in an intellectual class by herself— as Emerson was well aware. She wrote, in a letter to her friend Abba Francis,

> Eere long we shall be called to set our houses in
> order and go, we know not wither. But death is
> an event as natural as birth, and faith makes it as
> full of promise. But faith alas, is denied to certain
> minds, and submission must take its place. The
> Unknown, which lighted the morning of life will
> hallow and make serene its evening. Conscious or
> Unconscious we shall rest in the lap of the Infinite.

---

1   *Antony and Cleopatra*, Act V, Scene 2 (WS)
2   *To the Lighthouse,* Virginia Woolf

> Enough of this. Let us live while we live, and snatch
> each fleeting moment of truth and love and beauty.[1]

Could a philosophical response to the circumstance of our eventual deaths be stated more clearly and compactly?

Social Status

Societies stratify. They assign status ranks according to a variety of criteria. This may be unfair but it is a fact of life—a circumstance everyone feels and responds to. Birth, wealth, ethnic group, skin color, patterns of speech, and education are all factors that affect social status. Some of these we can change and some we are stuck with. Whitman recognized the existence of social ranks, but, naturally, he identified with all of them.

> Of every hue and caste am I, of every rank and
> religion,
> A farmer, mechanic, artist, gentleman, sailor, quaker,
> Prisoner, fancy-man, rowdy, lawyer, physician,
> priest.[2]

Shakespeare and his audience lived in a world sharply divided by social distinctions. In his plays, nobles were interesting but the commoners around them often had more sense. Kings and queens were at the top of the status heap but they rarely lived happily ever after. After Lear becomes insane his raving includes these lines about the uneven justice applied to persons of low and high status:

> Through tatter'd clothes small vices do appear;
> Robes and furr'd gowns hide all. Plate sin with gold,
> And the strong lance of justice hurtless breaks;
> Arm it in rags, a pygmy's straw does pierce it.[3]

To which the honorable Edgar exclaims, "Reason, in madness!"

---

1 *The Remarkable Mrs. Ripley,* Joan W. Goodwin
2 *Leaves of Grass,* Song of Myself (WW)
3 *King Lear,* Act IV, Scene 6 (WS)

Lust for power in their friends and relations causes Shakespeare's royals a great deal of trouble. In *Richard III* the queen complains,

> I had rather be a country servant-maid
> Than a great queen, with this condition,
> To be thus taunted, scorn'd, and baited at:
> Small joy have I in being England's queen.[1]

Emerson made many comments about social class. Sometimes he was democratic.

> If there is grandeur in you, you will find grandeur in porters and sweeps.[2]

Later in the same book he sounds snobbish.

> In the streets, we grow cynical. The men we meet are coarse and torpid. The finest wits have their sediment. What quantities of fribbles, paupers, invalids, epicures, antiquaries, politicians, thieves, and triflers of both sexes, might be advantageously spared! Mankind divides itself into two classes— benefactors and malefactors. The second class is vast, the first a handful.[3]

This is an example of the freedom Emerson awarded himself to write strongly stated contradictions. His inconsistency illuminates a complex attitude. He continued,

> Leave this hypocritical prating about the masses. Masses are rude, lame, unmade, pernicious in their demands and influence, and need not to be flattered but to be schooled. I wish not to concede anything to them, but to tame, drill, divide, and break them up, and draw individuals out of them. The worst of charity is, that the lives you are asked to preserve are not worth preserving. Masses! the calamity is the masses. I do not wish any

---

1   *Richard III*, Act 1, Scene 3 (WS)
2   *Conduct of Life*, Worship (RWE)
3   *Conduct of Life*, Considerations by the Way (RWE)

mass at all, but honest men only, lovely, sweet,
accomplished women only, and no shovel-handed,
narrow-brained, gin-drinking million stockingers or
lazzaroni at all. If government knew how, I should
like to see it check, not multiply the population.
When it reaches its true law of action, every man
that is born will be hailed as essential. Away
with this hurrah of masses, and let us have the
considerate vote of single men spoken on their
honor and their conscience. In old Egypt, it was
established law, that the vote of a prophet be
reckoned equal to a hundred hands. I think it was
much under-estimated.[1]

This was ugly social Darwinism. Why did Emerson allow it to get into print? But he went on to cheer upward mobility.

The wise workman will not regret the poverty
or the solitude which brought out his working
talents. The youth is charmed with the fine air and
accomplishments of the children of fortune. But all
great men come out of the middle classes.[2]

Emerson stated the egalitarian case this way.

As to what we call the masses, and common
men; — there are no common men. All men are
at last of a size; and true art is only possible, on
the conviction that every talent has its apotheosis
somewhere. Fair play, and an open field, and
freshest laurels to all who have won them! But
heaven reserves an equal scope for every creature.
Each is uneasy until he has produced his private
ray unto the concave sphere, and beheld his talent
also in its last nobility and exaltation.[3]

What we call obscure condition or vulgar society,
is that condition and society whose poetry is not
yet written, but which you shall presently make

---

1   *Conduct of Life,* Considerations by the Way (RWE)
2   *Conduct of Life,* Considerations by the Way (RWE)
3   *Representative Men,* Uses of Great Men (RWE)

as enviable and renowned as any. Accept your
genius, and say what you think.[1]

On this topic Emerson had stark internal conflicts. In some writings he was kinder to "the vulgar" than in others. Perhaps many high-status persons experience similar swings in their private estimates of people with less learning and less fortune than they have.

As though he knew in advance how African American culture would influence U.S. and world culture, Emerson wrote,

> Do you think the porter and the cook have no
> anecdotes, no experiences, no wonders for you?
> Everybody knows as much as the savant. The
> walls of rude minds are scrawled all over with
> facts, with thoughts. They shall one day bring a
> lantern and read the inscriptions. Every man, in the
> degree in which he has wit and culture, finds his
> curiosity inflamed concerning the modes of living
> and thinking of other men, and especially of those
> classes whose minds have not been subdued by
> the drill of school education.[2]

Social standing and wealth are related. Emerson's reform-minded companions were suspicious of property and other aspects of conventional American life.

> All our things are right and wrong together. The
> wave of evil washes all our institutions alike. Do
> you complain of our Marriage? Our marriage is
> no worse than our education, our diet, our trade,
> our social customs. Do you complain of the
> laws of Property? It is a pedantry to give such
> importance to them. Can we not play the game
> of life with these counters, as well as with those;
> in the institution of property, as well as out of it.
> Let into it the new and renewing principle of love,
> and property will be universality. No one gives the

---

1   *Essays,* Spiritual Laws (RWE)
2   *Essays,* Intellect (RWE)

impression of superiority to the institution, which he
must give who will reform it.[1]

The argument here is that our common ways of life, each
with proponents of reforming change, are no worse than
their alternatives; that what is needed to improve all of our
institutions is a greater infusion of kindness and fairness.
Easier proposed than accomplished.

Shakespeare had an egalitarian character suggest,

> So distribution should undo excess,
> And each man have enough.[2]

Emerson supported the profit motive.

> The division of labor, the multiplication of the arts
> of peace, which is nothing but a large allowance
> to each man to choose his work according to
> his faculty, — to live by his better hand, — fills
> the State with useful and happy laborers; and
> they, creating demand by the very temptation
> of their productions, are rapidly and surely
> rewarded by good sale: and what a police and ten
> commandments their work thus becomes! So true
> is Dr. Johnson's remark that men are seldom more
> innocently employed than when they are making
> money.[3]

He looked askance at un-earned wealth:

> A cultivated man becomes ashamed of his property,
> ashamed of what he has, out of new respect for his
> being. Especially he hates what he has, if he see
> that it is accidental, came to him by inheritance,
> or gift, or crime; then he feels that it is not having;
> it does not belong to him, has no root in him, and
> merely lies there, because no revolution or no
> robber takes it away.[4]

---

1   *Essays: Second Series,* New England Reformers (RWE)
2   *King Lear,* Act IV, Scene 1 (WS)
3   *Society and Solitude,* Civilization (RWE)
4   *Essays,* Self Reliance (RWE)

This is personal disclosure. Emerson benefited financially from his first wife's estate. He worked to earn his own money by lecturing and writing—and he was generous with cash assistance to friends such as the Alcott family. In the following he expresses his desire to play the benefactor.

> The love of wealth seems to grow chiefly out of the root of the love of the Beautiful. The desire of gold is not for gold. It is not the love of much wheat and wool and household-stuff. It is the means of freedom and benefit. We scorn shifts;[1] we desire the elegance of munificence; we desire at least to put no stint or limit on our parents, relatives, guests, or dependents; we desire to play the benefactor and the prince with our townsmen, with the stranger at the gate, with the bard, or the beauty, with the man or woman of worth, who alights at our door. How can we do this, if the wants of each day imprison us in lucrative labors, and constrain us to a continual vigilance lest we be betrayed into expense?[2]

In the end the Emersonian take on wealth was that internal assets such as learning, character, and devotion to ideals are more important than material riches. That was hardly a new insight in philosophy or religion—but Emerson expressed it with color and vigor.

> The pine and the oak shall gladly descend from the mountains to uphold the roof of men as faithful and necessary as themselves; to be the shelter always open to good and true persons; — a hall which shines with sincerity, brows ever tranquil, and a demeanor impossible to disconcert; whose inmates know what they want; who do not ask your house how theirs should be kept. They have aims: they cannot pause for trifles. The diet of the house does not create its order, but knowledge, character, action, absorb so much life and yield so much entertainment that the refectory has ceased

---

1   "Shifts" are petty economies.
2   *Society and Solitude,* Domestic Life (RWE)

to be so curiously studied. With a change of aim
has followed a change of the whole scale by which
men and things were wont to be measured. Wealth
and poverty are seen for what they are. It begins to
be seen that the poor are only they who feel poor,
and poverty consists in feeling poor. The rich, as we
reckon them, and among them the very rich, in a
true scale would be found very indigent and ragged.
The great make us feel, first of all, the indifference
of circumstances.[1]

We honor the rich because they have externally
the freedom, power and grace which we feel to be
proper to man, proper to us.[2]

Property, though, makes its own claims.

A man builds a fine house; and now he has a
master, and a task for life: he is to furnish, watch,
show it, and keep it in repair, the rest of his days.[3]

Whitman celebrated America's collective wealth but shared
the suspicion, common among non-affluent idealists, that
individual wealth is not admirable nor enviable.

Hast never come to thee an hour,
  A sudden gleam divine, precipitating, bursting all
these bubbles,
    fashions, wealth?
  These eager business aims—books, politics, art,
amours,
    To utter nothingness?[4]

Of persons arrived at high positions, ceremonies,
wealth,
    scholarships, and the like;
  (To me all that those persons have arrived at sinks
away from them,

---

1 *Society and Solitude,* Domestic Life (RWE)
2 *Essays,* History (RWE)
3 *Society and Solitude,* Works and Days (RWE)
4 *Leaves of Grass,* Hast never come to thee an hour (WW)

> except as it results to their bodies and souls,
> So that often to me they appear gaunt and naked,
> And often to me those men and women pass
> unwittingly the true
> realities of life, and go toward false realities,
> And often to me they are sad, hasty, unwaked
> sonnambules walking the dusk.)[1]

The rejoinder is that oft-quoted statement: "I've been rich and I've been poor. And, believe me, rich is better," which has been attributed to Mae West and others.

While the social class in which we grew up is a fated circumstance, our status within our circle of friends and acquaintances results from our own interactions.

> In every troop of boys that whoop and run in each
> yard and square, a new comer is as well and
> accurately weighed in the balance, in the course of
> a few days, and stamped with his right number, as
> if he had undergone a formal trial of his strength,
> speed, and temper.[2]

Emerson thought that the compulsion to define status and rank is inherent in people rather than unique to a particular culture and that it is innocent of ill-intent, flowing from human nature or from the nature of all social vertebrates. Perhaps there are exceptions but they are not wolves, chimpanzees, or dolphins. Fights use up energy and result in injuries, so behaviors that help animals avoid violent conflict are beneficial. Clear pecking orders are one such mechanism. Territorial boundaries, and respect for them, are another. Emerson expanded this idea in a later essay.

> When a new boy comes into school, when a man
> travels, and encounters strangers every day, or,
> when into any old club a newcomer is domesticated,
> that happens which befalls, when a strange ox is

---

1   *Leaves of Grass,* Thought (WW)
2   *Essays,* Spiritual Laws (RWE)

driven into a pen or pasture where cattle are kept; there is at once a trial of strength between the best pair of horns and the new comer, and it is settled thenceforth which is the leader. So now, there is a measuring of strength, very courteous, but decisive, and an acquiescence thenceforward when these two meet. Each reads his fate in the other's eyes. The weaker party finds, that none of his information or wit quite fits the occasion. He thought he knew this or that: he finds that he omitted to learn the end of it. Nothing that he knows will quite hit the mark, whilst all the rival's arrows are good, and well thrown. But if he knew all the facts in the encyclopaedia, it would not help him: for this is an affair of presence of mind, of attitude, of aplomb: the opponent has the sun and wind, and, in every cast, the choice of weapon and mark; and, when he himself is matched with some other antagonist, his own shafts fly well and hit. 'Tis a question of stomach and constitution. The second man is as good as the first, — perhaps better; but has not stoutness or stomach, as the first has, and so his wit seems over-fine or under-fine.[1]

Emerson thought he understood how social rank was determined.

Our fortunes in the world are as our mental equipment for this competition is. Yonder is a man who can answer the questions which I cannot. Is it so? Hence comes to me boundless curiosity to know his experiences and his wit. Hence competition for the stakes dearest to man. What is a match at whist, or draughts, or billiards, or chess, to a match of mother-wit, of knowledge, and of resources? However courteously we conceal it, it is social rank and spiritual power that are compared; whether in the parlor, the courts, the caucus, the senate, or the chamber of science, — which are only less or larger theatres for this competition.

---

1 *Conduct of Life,* Power (RWE)

> He that can define, he that can answer a question
> so as to admit of no further answer, is the best
> man.[1]

Place in Historical Time

Another circumstance we face, one common to all contemporaries, is where our lives fall in historical time. We do not grow up in the same culture as our ancestors. We have different technologies. The experimental method created a rigorous system of feedback that alters practical circumstances decade after decade. Emerson noted,

> Men love to wonder, and that is the seed of our
> science; and such is the mechanical determination
> of our age, and so recent are our best
> contrivances, that use has not dulled our joy and
> pride in them; and we pity our fathers for dying
> before steam and galvanism, sulphuric ether and
> ocean telegraphs, photograph and spectroscope
> arrived, as cheated out of half their human estate.
> These arts open great gates of a future, promising
> to make the world plastic and to lift human life out
> of its beggary to a godlike ease and power.

> Our century, to be sure, had inherited a tolerable
> apparatus. We had the compass, the printing-
> press, watches, the spiral spring, the barometer,
> the telescope. Yet so many inventions have been
> added, that life seems almost made over new...
> For the vast production and manifold application
> of iron is new; and our common and indispensable
> utensils of house and farm are new; the sewing-
> machine, the power-loom, the McCormick reaper,
> the mowing-machines, gas-light, lucifer matches,
> and the immense productions of the laboratory, are
> new in this century, and one franc's worth of coal
> does the work of a laborer for twenty days.[2]

---

1   *Society and Solitude,* Clubs (RWE)
2   *Society and Solitude,* Works and Days (RWE)

The pragmatic mainstream generally applauds technological advancement.

> Practical power. Men admire the man who can organize their wishes and thoughts in stone and wood and steel and brass, — the man who can build the boat, who has the impiety to make the rivers run the way he wants them, who can lead his telegraph through the ocean from shore to shore.[1]

Then as now, these changes had doubters and detractors. Emerson argued that progress was real and valuable.

> Readers of poetry see the factory-village, and the railway, and fancy that the poetry of the landscape is broken up by these; for these works of art are not yet consecrated in their reading; but the poet sees them fall within the great Order not less than the bee-hive, or the spider's geometrical web. Nature adopts them very fast into her vital circles, and the gliding train of cars she loves like her own.[2]

> I do not wish to look with sour aspect at the industrious manufacturing village, or the mart of commerce. I love the music of the water-wheel; I value the railway; I feel the pride which the sight of a ship inspires; I look on trade and every mechanical craft as education also.[3]

> The farmer had much ill-temper, laziness, and shirking to endure from his hand-sawyers, until one day he bethought him to put his saw-mill on the edge of a waterfall; and the river never tires of turning his wheel: the river is good-natured, and never hints an objection.[4]

Emerson noted progress in medicine.

---

1 *Society and Solitude,* Courage (RWE)
2 *Essays: Second Series,* The Poet (RWE)
3 *Addresses,* Method of Nature (RWE)
4 *Society and Solitude,* Civilization (RWE)

> How excellent are the mechanical aids we have applied to the human body, as in dentistry, in vaccination, in the rhinoplastic treatment; in the beautiful aid of ether, like a finer sleep...[1]

On computing, Emerson's showed his foresight.

> ... taught by Mr. Babbage[2], [technology] must calculate interest and logarithms. Lord Chancellor Thurlow[3] thought it might be made to draw bills and answers in chancery. If that were satire, it is yet coming to render many higher services of a mechanico-intellectual kind, and will leave the satire short of the fact.[4]

That has come to pass.

Emerson perceived that innovation is achieved collectively.

> It is easy to see that what is best written or done by genius, in the world, was no man's work, but came by wide social labor, when a thousand wrought like one, sharing the same impulse.[5]

Do such changes add up to progress?

> 'Tis too plain that with the material power the moral progress has not kept pace.
>
> No matter how many centuries of culture have preceded, the new man always finds himself standing on the brink of chaos, always in a crisis. Can anybody remember when the times were not hard, and money not scarce? Can anybody remember when sensible men, and the right sort of men, and the right sort of women, were plentiful?[6]

---

1   *Society and Solitude,* Works and Days (RWE)
2   Charles Babbage (1791-1871) and his collaborator, Ada Lovelace (1815-1852), were pioneers in digital computing and programing.
3   Edward Thurlow, 1st Baron Thurlow (1731–1806), a British lawyer and politician.
4   *Society and Solitude,* Works and Days (RWE)
5   *Representative Men,* Shakespeare; or, the Poet (RWE)
6   *Society and Solitude,* Works and Days (RWE)

Relationships

For most people the quantity of joy in their lives depends on the quality of their relationships. A few individuals can live sanely in isolation. The rest of us have social needs we address through family, romantic liaisons, friends, and co-workers. We nurture these relationships with conversation, collaboration, exchanges of care, shared activities—any way we can create companionship.

Family

One or more adults hold and feed every human infant. The first relationship of each human being is with the caregiving adults. Emerson wrote,

> The babe in arms is a channel through which the energies we call fate, love, and reason, visibly stream.[1]

The parents or their stand-ins set the terms of the relationship with the child. Grown-ups are larger, stronger, and control life's resources. *However,* Emerson noted,

> In my dealing with my child, my Latin and Greek, my accomplishments and my money, stead me nothing. They are all lost on him: but as much soul as I have, avails. If I am merely wilful, he gives me a Roland for an Oliver[2], sets his will against mine, one for one, and leaves me, if I please, the degradation of beating him by my superiority of strength. But if I renounce my will, and act for the soul, setting that up as umpire between us two, out of his young eyes looks the same soul; he reveres and loves with me.[3]

---

1   *Conduct of Life,* Considerations by the Way (RWE)
2   The phrase "a Roland for an Oliver" means a tit for tat, a blow for a blow. Roland, a legendary nephew of Charlemagne, fought Oliver to a draw in five days' single combat.
3   *Essays,* Oversoul (RWE)

This usage of *soul* means our emotional-ethical core, in which a balance of humility and strength stands ready for a trustful connection with another person. Emerson believed that young children are ready for this exchange. My experience agrees.

Here is another way Emerson wrote about the harmony of souls:

> If I put myself in the place of my child, and we
> stand in one thought, and see that things are thus
> or thus, that perception is law for him and me. We
> are both there, both act. But if, without carrying
> him into the thought, I look over into his plot, and,
> guessing how it is with him, ordain this or that, he
> will never obey me.[1]

Near the beginning of his poem-book, *Leaves of Grass*, Walt Whitman gives us a hint about the book's title, offering an image of a child clutching grass.

> A child said, What is the grass? fetching it to me
> with full hands;
> How could I answer the child? . . . . I do not know
> what it is any more than he.
> I guess it must be the flag of my disposition, out of
> hopeful green stuff woven.[2]

Humble uncertainty followed by readiness to share his thought—this is Whitman's way of *acting for the soul*. Candid humility undergirds all companionship. Emerson argued that children see through insincerity.

> Children are not deceived by the false reasons
> which their parents give in answer to their
> questions, whether touching natural facts, or
> religion, or persons. When the parent, instead
> of thinking how it really is, puts them off with a

---

1 *Essays: Second Series*, Politics (RWE)
2 *Leaves of Grass*, Song of Myself (WW)

traditional or a hypocritical answer, the children
perceive that it is traditional or hypocritical.[1]

Children learn from what they witness in the interactions
of people around them. Emerson said that the substance of this
learning could not be captured in language.

> The child amidst his baubles, is learning the action
> of light, motion, gravity, muscular force; and in the
> game of human life, love, fear, justice, appetite,
> man, and God, interact. These laws refuse to be
> adequately stated. They will not be written out on
> paper, or spoken by the tongue. They elude our
> persevering thought; yet we read them hourly in
> each other's faces, in each other's actions, in our
> own remorse.[2]

We do not choose our families, and we might not feel
particularly comfortable with the families we find ourselves
belonging to. Emerson put it this way:

> I cannot go to the houses of my nearest relatives,
> because I do not wish to be alone. Society exists by
> chemical affinity and not otherwise.[3]

Courtship

We are born into families, but we choose our romantic
partners. People have a deep fascination with characters and
situations involving the process of pairing up—stories such as
Pride and Prejudice.

> The strong bent of nature is seen in the proportion
> which this topic of personal relations usurps in
> the conversation of society. What do we wish to
> know of any worthy person so much as how he has
> sped in the history of this sentiment? What books
> in the circulating libraries circulate? How we glow
> over these novels of passion, when the story is

---

1   *Conduct of Life,* Worship (RWE)
2   *Addresses,* The Divinity School Address (RWE)
3   *Society and Solitude,* Society and Solitude (RWE)

told with any spark of truth and nature! And what fastens attention, in the intercourse of life, like any passage betraying affection between two parties? Perhaps we never saw them before, and never shall meet them again. But we see them exchange a glance, or betray a deep emotion, and we are no longer strangers. We understand them, and take the warmest interest in the development of the romance. All mankind love a lover.[1]

The tension between the power of sexual attraction and the reality of other considerations for selecting mates provides an ever-flowing source of plots and sub-plots for stories, and themes for preachy remarks. For example, in *Hamlet,* when Ophelia's brother takes his leave of his sister, he warns of the dangers posed by the desires of men who will do their best to stimulate passion in her.

> If with too credent ear you list his songs,
> Or lose your heart, or your chaste treasure open
> To his unmast'red importunity.
> Fear it, Ophelia, fear it, my dear sister,
> And keep you in the rear of your affection,
> Out of the shot and danger of desire.[2]

In *A Midsummer Night's Dream,* Shakespeare has Lysander list causes of turbulence in love. Hermia echoes with rhythmic re-phrasings.

> **Lysander.** Ay me! for aught that I could ever read,
> Could ever hear by tale or history,
> The course of true love never did run smooth;
> But, either it was different in blood, —
> **Hermia.** O cross! too high to be enthrall'd to low.
> **Lysander.** Or else misgraffed in respect of years, —
> **Hermia.** O spite! too old to be engaged to young.
> **Lysander.** Or else it stood upon the choice of friends, —

---

1   *Essays,* Love (RWE)
2   *Hamlet,* Act I, Scene 3 (WS)

Hermia. O hell! to choose love by another's eyes.
Lysander. Or, if there were a sympathy in choice,
War, death, or sickness did lay siege to it,
Making it momentary as a sound,
Swift as a shadow, short as any dream;
Brief as the lightning in the collied night,
That, in a spleen, unfolds both heaven and earth,
And ere a man hath power to say 'Behold!'
The jaws of darkness do devour it up:
So quick bright things come to confusion.
Hermia. If then true lovers have been ever cross'd,
It stands as an edict in destiny:
Then let us teach our trial patience,
Because it is a customary cross,
As due to love as thoughts and dreams and sighs,
Wishes and tears, poor fancy's followers.[1]

The strategies of courtship are a theme in another of Shakespeare's plays. Cressida has pretended indifference to Troilus, but when she's left alone she informs the audience,

Things won are done; joy's soul lies in the doing.
That she beloved knows nought that knows not
this:
Men prize the thing ungain'd more than it is:
That she was never yet that ever knew
Love got so sweet as when desire did sue.
Therefore this maxim out of love I teach:
Achievement is command; ungain'd, beseech:
Then though my heart's content firm love doth bear,
Nothing of that shall from mine eyes appear.[2]

Love's Labor Lost has a simple plot. A king and three noblemen vow to spend three years apart from women, immersed in study. The daughter of a neighboring king and three ladies arrive for a diplomatic meeting—the king had forgotten about this appointment when he made his vow.

---

1   *A Midsummer Night's Dream*, Act I Scene 1 (WS)
2   *Troilus and Cressida*, Act I, Scene 2 (WS)

Each man falls in love with one of the four women. They all write corny love letters, but because of their oaths, none tells the others of his new passion. Their mutual secrecy is soon exploded. Ashamed to have broken their word, they turn to their intellectual leader, Biron, to justify their behavior, which he does, in a speech that includes the following:

> But love, first learned in a lady's eyes,
> Lives not alone immured in the brain;
> But, with the motion of all elements,
> Courses as swift as thought in every power,
> And gives to every power a double power,
> Above their functions and their offices.
> It adds a precious seeing to the eye;
> A lover's eyes will gaze an eagle blind;
> A lover's ear will hear the lowest sound,
> Love's feeling is more soft and sensible
> Than are the tender horns of cockl'd snails;
> Love's tongue proves dainty Bacchus gross in
> taste:
> For valour, is not Love a Hercules,
> Still climbing trees in the Hesperides?
> Subtle as Sphinx; as sweet and musical
> As bright Apollo's lute, strung with his hair:
> And when Love speaks, the voice of all the gods
> Makes heaven drowsy with the harmony.
> Never durst poet touch a pen to write
> Until his ink were temper'd with Love's sighs;
> O, then his lines would ravish savage ears
> And plant in tyrants mild humility.
> From women's eyes this doctrine I derive:
> They sparkle still the right Promethean fire;
> They are the books, the arts, the academes,
> That show, contain and nourish all the world.[1]

Perhaps Emerson was inspired by Biron's speech when he wrote:

---

1   *Love's Labor Lost,* Act IV, Scene 3 (WS)

> And what is specially true of love is, that it is a state
> of extreme impressionability; the lover has more
> senses and finer senses than others; his eye and
> ear are telegraphs; he reads omens on the flower,
> and cloud, and face, and form, and gesture, and
> reads them aright. In his surprise at the sudden
> and entire understanding that is between him
> and the beloved person, it occurs to him that
> they might somehow meet independently of time
> and place. How delicious the belief that he could
> elude all guards, precautions, ceremonies, means,
> and delays, and hold instant and sempiternal
> communication![1]

Emerson called the experience of falling in love *the enchantment of human life*.

> Nature, uncontainable, flowing, fore-looking, in the
> first sentiment of kindness anticipates already a
> benevolence which shall lose all particular regards
> in its general light. The introduction to this felicity is
> in a private and tender relation of one to one, which
> is the enchantment of human life.
>
> It is to be considered that this passion of which
> we speak, though it begin with the young, yet
> forsakes not the old, or rather suffers no one who
> is truly its servant to grow old, but makes the aged
> participators of it, not less than the tender maiden,
> though in a different and nobler sort. For, it is a fire
> that kindling its first embers in the narrow nook of
> a private bosom, caught from a wandering spark
> out of another private heart, glows and enlarges
> until it warms and beams upon multitudes of men
> and women, upon the universal heart of all, and
> so lights up the whole world and all nature with its
> generous flames. It matters not, therefore, whether
> we attempt to describe the passion at twenty, at
> thirty, or at eighty years.[2]

Emerson returned to the wonderful spell of the crush.

---

1 *Society and Solitude,* Success (RWE)
2 *Essays,* Love (RWE)

Thus even love, which is the deification of persons, must become more impersonal every day. Of this at first it gives no hint. Little think the youth and maiden who are glancing at each other across crowded rooms, with eyes so full of mutual intelligence, of the precious fruit long hereafter to proceed from this new, quite external stimulus. . . . From exchanging glances, they advance to acts of courtesy, of gallantry, then to fiery passion, to plighting troth and marriage. Passion beholds its object as a perfect unit. The soul is wholly embodied, and the body is wholly ensouled.[1]

Margaret Fuller offered this instruction:

To you, women of America, it is more especially my business to address myself on this subject, and my advice may be classed under three heads:

Clear your souls from the taint of vanity.

Do not rejoice in conquests, either that your power to allure may be seen by other women, or for the pleasure of rousing passionate feelings that gratify your love of excitement.

It must happen, no doubt, that frank and generous women will excite love they do not reciprocate, but, in nine cases out of ten, the woman has, half consciously, done much to excite. In this case, she shall not be held guiltless, either as to the unhappiness or injury of the lover. Pure love, inspired by a worthy object, must ennoble and bless, whether mutual or not; but that which is excited by coquettish attraction of any grade of refinement, must cause bitterness and doubt, as to the reality of human goodness, so soon as the flush of passion is over.

And, that you may avoid all taste for these false pleasures,

"Steep the soul

In one pure love, and it will last thee long."[2]

---

1   *Essays,* Love (RWE)
2   *Woman in the Nineteenth Century,* Margaret Fuller

In the best case, thought Emerson, the excitement of early love is succeeded by a serene companionship, as between fond siblings.

> When all is done, a person of related mind, a
> brother or sister by nature, comes to us so softly
> and easily, so nearly and intimately, as if it were the
> blood in our proper veins, that we feel as if some
> one was gone, instead of another having come:
> we are utterly relieved and refreshed: it is a sort of
> joyful solitude.[1]

Marriage

Both Shakespeare and Emerson wrote about the difference between the longing for love and the result of its attainment. *Having* a husband and *being* a spouse alter each partner's perception of the other—so wrote Emerson, and he said there was no help for it.

> What avails it to fight with the eternal laws of mind,
> which adjust the relation of all persons to each
> other, by the mathematical measure of their havings
> and beings? Gertrude is enamored of Guy; how
> high, how aristocratic, how Roman his mien and
> manners! To live with him were life indeed: and no
> purchase is too great; and heaven and earth are
> moved to that end. Well, Gertrude has Guy: but
> what now avails how high, how aristocratic, how
> Roman his mien and manners, if his heart and aims
> are in the senate, in the theatre, and in the billiard
> room, and she has no aims, no conversation that
> can enchant her graceful lord?[2]

Romantic stories end when difficulties and misunderstandings are overcome and the important pair bonds gel. Cinderella and her prince join hands, and all is well; Elizabeth and Mr. Darcy settle things with mutual happiness. Marriage is presumed to follow. Then the foundation of

---

1 *Essays,* Spiritual Laws (RWE)
2 *Essays,* Spiritual Laws (RWE)

passionate attraction faces the tests of days and moods, of duties and chores, and of misaligned expectations, resulting in some mixture of satisfaction with disappointment and frustration. Shakespeare's characters often expressed skepticism about marriage.

Rosalind. Now tell me how long you would have her, after you have possess'd her.
Orlando. For ever and a day.
Rosalind. Say 'a day' without the 'ever.' No, no, Orlando; men are April when they woo, December when they wed: maids are May when they are maids, but the sky changes when they are wives. I will be more jealous of thee than a Barbary cock-pigeon over his hen, more clamorous than a parrot against rain, more new-fangled than an ape, more giddy in my desires than a monkey. I will weep for nothing, like Diana in the fountain, and I will do that when you are dispos'd to be merry; I will laugh like a hyena, and that when thou are inclin'd to sleep.[1]

Domitius Enobarus. Why, sir, give the gods a thankful sacrifice. When it pleaseth their deities to take the wife of a man from him, it shows to man the tailors of the earth; comforting therein, that when old robes are worn out, there are members to make new. If there were no more women but Fulvia, then had you indeed a cut, and the case to be lamented: this grief is crowned with consolation; your old smock brings forth a new petticoat: and indeed the tears live in an onion that should water this sorrow.[2]

Cleopatra. Why should I think you can be mine and true,
Though you in swearing shake the throned gods,
Who have been false to Fulvia? Riotous madness,

---

1 *As You Like It*, Act IV, Scene 1 (WS)
2 *Antony and Cleopatra*, Act I, Scene 2 (WS)

To be entangled with those mouth-made vows,
Which break themselves in swearing![1]

Slender. I will marry her, sir, at your request: but if
there be no great love in the beginning, yet heaven
may decrease it upon better acquaintance, when
we are married and have more occasion to know
one another;
I hope, upon familiarity will grow more contempt.[2]

Margaret Fuller published *Woman in the Nineteenth Century*
in 1845, in which she describes styles of marriage:

First; -- The household partnership. In our country,
the woman looks for a "smart but kind" husband;
the man for a "capable, sweet-tempered" wife. The
man furnishes the house; the woman regulates
it. Their relation is one of mutual esteem, mutual
dependence. Their talk is of business; their
affection shows itself by practical kindness. Each
for the other's aid; they are grateful and content.
The wife praises her husband as a "good provider";
the husband, in return, compliments her as a
"capital housekeeper." This relation is good so far
as it goes.

Next comes a closer tie, which takes the form either
of mutual idolatry or of intellectual companionship.
The first, we suppose, is to no one a pleasing
subject of contemplation. The parties weaken and
narrow one another; they lock the gate against all
the glories of the universe, that they may live in a
cell together. To themselves they seem the only
wise; to all others, steeped in infatuation; the gods
smile as they look forward to the crisis of cure;
to men, the woman seems an unlovely syren; to
women, the man an effeminate boy.

The other form, of intellectual companionship,
has become more and more frequent. Men
engaged in public life, literary men, and artists,

---

1   *Antony and Cleopatra*, Act I, Scene 3 (WS)
2   *Merry Wives of Windsor*, Act I, Scene 1 (WS)

have often found in their wives companions and confidants in thought no less than in feeling. And, as the intellectual development of Woman has spread wider and risen higher, they have, not unfrequently, shared the same employment; as in the case of Roland[1] and his wife, who were friends in the household and in the nation's councils, read, regulated home affairs, or prepared public documents together, indifferently. It is very pleasant, in letters begun by Roland and finished by his wife, to see the harmony of mind, and the difference of nature; one thought, but various ways of treating it.[2]

Margaret Fuller's observations about marriage preceded her own domestic partnership, which was cut short by shipwreck. It would have been instructive to read what she learned from raising a child and living with her husband. Unfortunately they all died off Long Island in 1850 at the end of her attempted return from Italy.

Fuller's friend Emerson offered these thoughts about the maturation of a marital relationship:

Their once flaming regard is sobered by time in either breast, and losing in violence what it gains in extent, it becomes a thorough good understanding. They resign each other, without complaint, to the good offices which man and woman are severally appointed to discharge in time, and exchange the passion which once could not lose sight of its object, for a cheerful, disengaged furtherance, whether present or absent, of each other's designs. At last they discover that all which at first drew them together, those once sacred features, that magical play of

---

1   This is a different Roland—not the mythical warrior mentioned earlier. Here Fuller refers to Jean-Marie Roland de la Platière, whose well-educated wife, Madame Roland, was a partner in his work. After she was martyred in the French Revolution's Terror, Roland committed suicide.

2   *Woman in the Nineteenth Century,* Margaret Fuller

charms, was deciduous, had a prospective end, like the scaffolding by which the house was built.[1]

It is interesting that Emerson included the word "disengaged," declining the notion of the two becoming one. If disengaged, the two remain two, with trust in reliable support from their partner. If they don't have that, they might as well part ways—as many do.

Emerson had harsh words for the idea of one spouse demanding love from the other.

> I know how delicious is this cup of love, — I existing for you, you existing for me; but it is a child's clinging to his toy; an attempt to eternize the fireside and nuptial chamber; to keep the picture-alphabet through which our first lessons are prettily conveyed.

> Far from there being anything divine in the low and proprietary sense of "Do you love me?" it is only when you leave and lose me, by casting yourself on a sentiment which is higher than both of us, that I draw near, and find myself at your side; and I am repelled, if you fix your eye on me, and demand love.[2]

Sometimes Emerson called the whole arrangement into doubt.

> Is not marriage an open question, when it is alleged, from the beginning of the world, that such as are in the institution wish to get out, and such as are out wish to get in?[3]

> A youth marries in haste; afterwards, when his mind is opened to the reason of the conduct of life, he is asked, what he thinks of the institution of marriage, and of the right relations of the sexes? "I should have much to say," he might reply, "if the question

---

1 *Essays*, Love (RWE)
2 *Representative Men*, Swedenborg; or, the Mystic (RWE)
3 *Representative Men*, Montaigne; or, the Skeptic (RWE)

> were open, but I have a wife and children, and all
> question is closed for me."[1]

> Nothing is secure but life, transition, the energizing
> spirit. No love can be bound by oath or covenant
> to secure it against a higher love. No truth so
> sublime but it may be trivial tomorrow in the light
> of new thoughts. People wish to be settled: only
> as far as they are unsettled, is there any hope for
> them.[2]

Misgivings about marriage appeared in his writing, but in
life Emerson married twice, and stayed married, in both cases,
until death brought separation.

> We are not very much to blame for our bad
> marriages. We live amid hallucinations; and this
> especial trap is laid to trip up our feet with, and all
> are tripped up first or last. But the mighty Mother
> who had been so sly with us, as if she felt that
> she owed us some indemnity, insinuates into the
> Pandora-box of marriage some deep and serious
> benefits, and some great joys. We find a delight
> in the beauty and happiness of children, that
> makes the heart too big for the body. In the worst-
> assorted connections there is ever some mixture
> of true marriage.[3]

The closing sentences of this paragraph are euphonic. In
his biography of Emerson, James Marcus calls out this element
of Emerson's style, the rap-rap-rap of single-syllable words
("that makes the heart too big for the body" sandwiched
between poly-syllabic words ("worst-assorted connections").

If we are patient, determined, and fortunate we connect
ourselves to others and live suspended in a web of positive
relationships. Nonetheless each of us, in some fundamental
ways, remains alone.

---

1   *English Traits*, Religion (RWE)
2   *Essays*, Circles (RWE)
3   *Conduct of Life*, Illusions (RWE)

> Though the stuff of tragedy and of romances is
> in a moral union of two superior persons, whose
> confidence in each other for long years, out of
> sight, and in sight, and against all appearances,
> is at last justified by victorious proof of probity to
> gods and men, causing joyful emotions, tears and
> glory, — though there be for heroes this moral
> union, yet, they, too, are as far off as ever from
> an intellectual union, and the moral union is for
> comparatively low and external purposes, like the
> co-operation of a ship's company or of a fire-club.
> But how insular and pathetically solitary are all the
> people we know![1]

That said, Emerson signed off on this topic with a ringing endorsement of marriage, contingent on a foundation *formed from character*.

> Happy will that house be in which the relations are
> formed from character, after the highest, and not
> after the lowest order; the house in which character
> marries, and not confusion and a miscellany of
> unavowable motives. Then shall marriage be a
> covenant to secure to either party the sweetness
> and honor of being a calm, continuing, inevitable
> benefactor to the other.[2]

With good will and good fortune, spouses are good friends.

Friendship

We hope for, and prize, friendship as a component of family and romantic relationships, because that means they include the rewards of companionship and conversation. Conversation is the activity most fundamental to friendship, although we should allow for the importance of various forms of parallel play, not only in the usual sense enjoyed by young children but also encompassing fishing buddies and bridge partners and other activities done together, without much verbiage required.

---

1   *Society and Solitude,* Society and Solitude (RWE)
2   *Society and Solitude,* Domestic Life (RWE)

Emerson had a great deal to say about friendship, starting with the essay of that title in his first book and continuing in later works. Usually, he emphasized how important friendships were to him, but sometimes he complained about being disappointed. These let-downs were mostly with reference to the intellectual companionship for which he hungered. He cherished honesty and mutual care.

> A friend is a person with whom I may be sincere. Before him, I may think aloud. I am arrived at last in the presence of a man so real and equal, that I may drop even those undermost garments of dissimulation, courtesy, and second thought, which men never put off, and may deal with him with the simplicity and wholeness, with which one chemical atom meets another. Sincerity is the luxury allowed, like diadems and authority, only to the highest rank, that being permitted to speak truth, as having none above it to court or conform unto. Every man alone is sincere. At the entrance of a second person, hypocrisy begins.

> The other element of friendship is Tenderness. We are holden to men by every sort of tie, by blood, by pride, by fear, by hope, by lucre, by lust, by hate, by admiration, by every circumstance and badge and trifle, but we can scarce believe that so much character can subsist in another as to draw us by love. Can another be so blessed, and we so pure, that we can offer him tenderness? When a man becomes dear to me, I have touched the goal of fortune. I find very little written directly to the heart of this matter in books.[1]

A tension exists between these two elements of friendship. Tenderness and frankness are often at odds. That's why "hypocrisy" begins—but he needn't have used such a harsh word for the moments when our kindness overrides our candor. In the next paragraph Emerson continues his line of thought about this difficulty:

---

1   *Essays,* Friendship (RWE)

> Friendship requires that rare mean betwixt likeness
> and unlikeness, that piques each with the presence
> of power and of consent in the other party. Let me
> be alone to the end of the world, rather than that my
> friend should overstep by a word or a look his real
> sympathy. I am equally baulked by antagonism and
> by compliance. Let him not cease an instant to be
> himself.
>
> We foolishly think, in our days of sin, that we must
> court friends by compliance to the customs of
> society, to its dress, its breeding and its estimates.
> But later, if we are so happy, we learn that only that
> soul can be my friend, which I encounter on the
> line of my own march, that soul to which I do not
> decline, and which does not decline to me, but,
> native of the same celestial latitude, repeats in its
> own all my experience.
>
> The end of friendship is a commerce the most strict
> and homely that can be joined; more strict than
> any of which we have experience. It is for aid and
> comfort through all the relations and passages of
> life and death. It is fit for serene days, and graceful
> gifts, and country rambles, but also for rough roads
> and hard fare, shipwreck, poverty, and persecution.[1]

No actual friend (or spouse or parent) rings all those bells, but we don't expect them to. We wish that each friendship bring us something sturdy, encouraging, instructive or otherwise helpful. We look to the sum of these relationships as a chief support of mental health. The flow of information through such channels sustains every aspect of well-being, as does the flow of care.

Expanding on the worth of friendship, Emerson wrote,

> I know nothing which life has to offer so satisfying
> as the profound good understanding, which can
> subsist, after much exchange of good offices,

---

1 *Essays,* Friendship (RWE)

> between two virtuous men, each of whom is sure
> of himself, and sure of his friend.[1]

> This is the service of a friend. With him we are
> easily great. There is a sublime attraction in him
> to whatever virtue is in us. How he flings wide the
> doors of existence! What questions we ask of him!
> what an understanding we have! How few words
> are needed! It is the only real society. And yet we
> do not provide for the greatest good of life. We
> take care of our health; we lay up money; we make
> our roof tight, and our clothing sufficient; but who
> provides wisely that he shall not be wanting in the
> best property of all, — friends?[2]

> We talk of choosing our friends, but friends are
> self-elected. Reverence is a great part of it. Treat
> your friend as a spectacle. Of course, if he be a
> man, he has merits that are not yours, and that you
> cannot honor, if you must needs hold him close to
> your person. Stand aside. Give those merits room.
> … Leave it to girls and boys to regard a friend as
> property.[3]

Emerson described the nurture that friendship requires
and deserves.

> Friendship should be surrounded with ceremonies
> and respects, and not crushed into corners.
> Friendship requires more time than poor busy men
> can usually command.[4]

He prescribed patience.

> We say, that every man is entitled to be valued by
> his best moment. We measure our friends so. We
> know, they have intervals of folly, whereof we take
> no heed, but wait the reappearings of the genius,
> which are sure and beautiful.[5]

---

1   *Essays: Second Series,* Character (RWE)
2   *Conduct of Life,* Considerations by the Way (RWE)
3   *Essays,* Friendship (RWE)
4   *Conduct of Life,* Behavior (RWE)
5   *Conduct of Life,* Beauty (RWE)

That is from *Conduct of Life,* which Emerson published nearly twenty years after his essay on friendship. During those decades his expectations of his friends came down to earth.

The following point is of interest because a secret voice that desires social status and rich diversion *whispers,* from time to time, that our circle of friends should include more individuals of higher attainment, or higher *something.* Apparently it was the same with Emerson.

> Let us suck the sweetness of those affections and consuetudes that grow near us. These old shoes are easy to the feet. Undoubtedly, we can easily pick faults in our company, can easily whisper names prouder, and that tickle the fancy more. Every man's imagination hath its friends; and pleasant would life be with such companions. But, if you cannot have them on good mutual terms, you cannot have them.[1]

What friendships did Emerson covet? Who would he have invited to his imaginary dinner party, had he played that game?

It is our social bonds rather than our intellects that allow us to feel that our lives matter more than the shadow of a cloud passing over a pond. Most friendships result from and grow through conversation, and all intellectual friendships do so. Conversation involves talk with its forms and attributes, body language, and everything we express through gestures and facial expressions. Emerson thought that the process of talking creates an intellectual pecking order.

> Put any company of people together with freedom for conversation, and a rapid self-distribution takes place, into sets and pairs. The best are accused of exclusiveness. It would be more true to say, they separate as oil from water, as children from old people, without love or hatred in the matter, each seeking his like; and any interference with the

---

1   *Essays,* Prudence (RWE)

affinities would produce constraint and suffocation. All conversation is a magnetic experiment.[1]

As soon as the stranger begins to intrude his partialities, his definitions, his defects, into the conversation, it is all over. He has heard the first, the last and best, he will ever hear from us. He is no stranger now. Vulgarity, ignorance, misapprehension, are old acquaintances. Now, when he comes, he may get the order, the dress, and the dinner, but the throbbing of the heart, and the communications of the soul, no more.[2]

Ach! To be found unworthy...

As writing has various purposes, so does conversation.

We seek society with very different aims, and the staple of conversation is widely unlike in its circles. Sometimes it is facts, — running from those of daily necessity to the last results of science, and has all degrees of importance; sometimes it is love, and makes the balm of our early and of our latest days; sometimes it is thought, as from a person who is a mind only; sometimes a singing, as if the heart poured out all like a bird; sometimes experience. With some men it is a debate; at the approach of a dispute they neigh like horses. Unless there be an argument, they think nothing is doing. Some talkers excel in the precision with which they formulate their thoughts, so that you get from them somewhat to remember; others lay criticism asleep by a charm.[3]

Madame de Staël lusted for good conversation.

The kind of pleasure that a lively conversation affords does not precisely consist in its subject; neither the ideas nor the knowledge it unfolds are its main interest. Rather, it is a certain way of interacting, of giving mutual and immediate

---

1   *Society and Solitude,* Society and Solitude (RWE)
2   *Essays,* Friendship (RWE)
3   *Society and Solitude,* Clubs (RWE)

pleasure, of speaking at the moment you think,
of enjoying oneself instantly, of gaining approval
effortlessly, of revealing your understanding in all
its nuances by accent, gesture, look—in short, of
stimulating spontaneity like a kind of electricity
that makes sparks fly, relieving some people of
their excess of vitality and wakening others from
oppressive apathy.[1]

French conversation exists only in Paris, and
conversation has been my greatest pleasure since
childhood. I was so emotionally upset by the fear
of being deprived of this visit that reason was
powerless to help me. I was overflowing with zest
for life at that time; and it is precisely the need
for intense pleasures which most often leads to
despair, for it makes resignation—without which one
cannot bear life's vicissitudes —very difficult.[2]

Emerson read de Staël and shared her enthusiasm. De Staël
loved Paris. Emerson mentioned the great English-speaking
metropolises.

Cities give us collision. 'Tis said, London and New
York take the nonsense out of a man. A great part of
our education is sympathetic and social.[3]

Novels were considered light reading, or worse, in
Emerson's time, and he sometimes joined in scorning them.
But he allowed they had merit with respect to conversation.

The novels are as useful as Bibles, if they teach
you the secret, that the best of life is conversation,
and the greatest success is confidence, or perfect
understanding between sincere people. The highest
compact we can make with our fellow, is, — 'Let
there be truth between us two forevermore.'[4]

1 *Madame de Staël on Politics, Literature, and National Character,*
   Madame de Staël
2 *Ten Years of Exile,* Madame de Staël
3 *Conduct of Life,* Culture (RWE)
4 *Conduct of Life,* Behavior (RWE)

Emerson had one rule he wished us to note.

> There is one topic peremptorily forbidden to all
> well-bred, to all rational mortals, namely, their
> distempers. If you have not slept, or if you have
> slept, or if you have head-ache, or sciatica, or
> leprosy, or thunder-stroke, I beseech you, by all
> angels, to hold your peace, and not pollute the
> morning, to which all the housemates bring serene
> and pleasant thoughts, by corruption and groans.[1]

Sometimes we encounter people who are fountains of talk. It is always their turn to serve. Their flow of speech has few breaks, and if someone else does get in a remark, they find a way to take back the floor. They don't seem interested in others either because they *aren't* interested or because they lack the knack of showing it. This does not make for good conversation.

Conversation is a particular species of verbal exchange. There are others; we human beings interact through language in many ways. We tease, bargain, instruct, complain, pass information, and flatter.

> Men use to tell us that we love flattery, even
> though we are not deceived by it, because it
> shows that we are of importance enough to be
> courted.[2]

And we gossip.

> A scholar does not wish to be always pumping his
> brains: he wants gossips.[3]

Sometimes Emerson used the word *scholar* where we would say *writer*. A writer wants to hear gossip because he or she is interested in the private concerns and doings of people,

---

1   *Conduct of Life*, Behavior (RWE)
2   *Essays: Second Series*, Gifts (RWE)
3   *Society and Solitude*, Clubs (RWE)

not just in their opinions and knowledge. The more private, the more interesting.

Another subhead of talk is *advice.* In *Hamlet,* Shakespeare has an old man named Polonius make a speech to his son, who is about to leave for a long trip.

> My blessing with thee! And these few precepts in
> thy memory.
> Look thou character. Give thy thoughts no tongue,
> Nor any unproportion'd thought his act.
> Be thou familiar, but by no means vulgar:
> Those friends thou hast, and their adoption tried,
> Grapple them unto thy soul with hoops of steel;
> But do not dull thy palm with entertainment
> Of each new-hatch'd, unfledg'd comrade. Beware
> Of entrance to a quarrel; but being in,
> Bear't that th' opposed may beware of thee.
> Give every man thine ear, but few thy voice;
> Take each man's censure, but reserve thy judgment.
> Costly thy habit as thy purse can buy,
> But not express'd in fancy; rich, not gaudy;
> For the apparel oft proclaims the man,
> And they in France of the best rank and station
> Are most select and generous, chief in that.
> Neither a borrower nor a lender be;
> For loan oft loses both itself and friend,
> And borrowing dulls the edge of husbandry.
> This above all- to thine own self be true,
> And it must follow, as the night the day,
> Thou canst not then be false to any man.[1]

An Emersonian closing, for sure. And Emerson supported his needy friends with gifts rather than loans.

Polonius's basket of advice includes advice about advice: "Give every man thine ear, but few thy voice." Emerson expressed skepticism about the value of advice.

---

1   *Hamlet,* Act I, Scene 3 (WS)

> Although this garrulity of advising is born with us, I
> confess that life is rather a subject of wonder, than
> of didactics. So much fate, so much irresistible
> dictation from temperament and unknown
> inspiration enters into it, that we doubt we can say
> anything out of our own experience whereby to
> help each other.[1]

Duty

Duties stem from relationships, because each is a duty *to*. Here is Emerson's reflection on this subject:

> Consider whether you have satisfied your relations
> to father, mother, cousin, neighbor, town, cat, and
> dog; whether any of these can upbraid you. But I
> may also neglect this reflex standard, and absolve
> me to myself. I have my own stern claims and
> perfect circle. It denies the name of duty to many
> offices that are called duties. But if I can discharge
> its debts, it enables me to dispense with the
> popular code. If any one imagines that this law is
> lax, let him keep its commandment one day.[2]

I like the way Emerson moved from a list of ordinary obligations to allowing that he might define his duties by his own light. He closes by daring a hypothetical critic to live up to his self-imposed standard.

Competition and Leadership

> Nobody is glad in the gladness of another, and our
> system is one of war, of an injurious superiority.
> Every child of the Saxon race is educated to wish
> to be first. It is our system; and a man comes
> to measure his greatness by the regrets, envies,
> and hatreds of his competitors. But in these new
> fields there is room: here are no self-esteems, no
> exclusions.[3]

---

1   *Conduct of Life,* Considerations by the Way (RWE)
2   *Essays,* Self Reliance (RWE)
3   *Representative Men,* Uses of Great Men (RWE)

Judge for yourself to what degree the first three sentences are true. We could apply the phrase *these new fields* to recent history, noting big rewards for skill with technology. People who, in earlier decades, might have been oddball ne'er-do-wells, in the digital age became sought-after computer programmers. Technology made room for all types of nerds and proved that success is not a zero-sum game. Coders can work independently, without a supervisor looking over their shoulders. Some temperaments will go to great lengths to avoid having a boss—and everyone, I suppose, chafes under control by others. Emerson wrote,

> Whilst I do what is fit for me, and abstain from what is unfit, my neighbor and I shall often agree in our means, and work together for a time to one end. But whenever I find my dominion over myself not sufficient for me, and undertake the direction of him also, I overstep the truth, and come into false relations to him.[1]

Although we squirm when we feel someone trying to control us, the coordination of group efforts requires leadership, which is complex and difficult. Emerson tipped his hat to those who are good at it.

> To the leaders of men, the brain as well as the flesh and the heart must furnish a proportion. Defect in manners is usually the defect of fine perceptions.[2]

> These men correct the delirium of the animal spirits, make us considerate, and engage us to new aims and powers. The veneration of mankind selects these for the highest place.

> I like a master standing firm on legs of iron, well-born, rich, handsome, eloquent, loaded with advantages, drawing all men by fascination into tributaries and supporters of his power. Sword and

---

1 *Essays: Second Series*, Politics (RWE)
2 *Essays: Second Series*, Manners (RWE)

staff, or talents sword-like or staff-like, carry on
the work of the world. But I find him greater, when
he can abolish himself, and all heroes, by letting
in this element of reason, irrespective of persons;
this subtiliser, and irresistible upward force, into
our thought, destroying individualism; the power
so great, that the potentate is nothing. Then he is
a monarch, who gives a constitution to his people;
a pontiff, who preaches the equality of souls,
and releases his servants from their barbarous
homages; an emperor, who can spare his empire.[1]

----

1   *Representative Men,* Uses of Great Men (RWE)

Feelings

Many passages in Emerson's essays are about emotions or emotionally-charged attitudes. He often uses lively imagery to make his points. For example, instead of simply remarking that human beings are animals, who behave as hominids regardless of formalities they affect, Emerson wrote:

> We talk of deviations from natural life, as if artificial life were not also natural. The smoothest curled courtier in the boudoirs of a palace has an animal nature, rude and aboriginal as a white bear, omnipotent to its own ends, and is directly related, there amid essences and billets doux,[1] to Himmaleh mountain-chains, and the axis of the globe.[2]

Acquaintances sometimes concluded that Emerson, influenced as he was by the style of 19th century New England, was rather chilly. Perhaps he seemed so, but he praised emotional vigor.

> 'T is not new facts that avail, but the heat to dissolve everybody's facts. Heat puts you in right relation with magazines of facts. The capital defect of cold, arid natures is the want of animal spirits. They seem a power incredible, as if God should raise the dead. Animal spirits constitute the power of the present, and their feats are like the structure of a pyramid. Their result is a lord, a general, or a boon companion.[3]

Emerson sought a flow of vivacity in his friends and thought that enthusiasm led to success in every realm. At the same time, his experience of life made him aware that animal spirits bring people into danger.

---

1 "billets doux" – love letters
2 *Essays,* Self-Reliance (RWE)
3 *Society and Solitude,* Society and Solitude (RWE)

> Men of this surcharge of arterial blood cannot live
> on nuts, herb-tea, and elegies; cannot read novels,
> and play whist; cannot satisfy all their wants at the
> Thursday Lecture, or the Boston Athenaeum. They
> pine for adventure, and must go to Pike's Peak;
> had rather die by the hatchet of a Pawnee, than
> sit all day and every day at a counting-room desk.
> They are made for war, for the sea, for mining,
> hunting, and clearing; for hair-breadth adventures,
> huge risks, and the joy of eventful living.[1]

Emerson hypothesized that evolution had permitted risk-taking to assure related benefits. Darwin's *Origin of Species* shook the intellectual world on its publication in 1859; the following was published in 1870.

> Nature secures the execution of her aim, drops off.
> To keep man in the planet, she impresses the terror
> of death. To perfect the commissariat, she implants
> in each a certain rapacity to get the supply, and
> a little oversupply, of his wants. To insure the
> existence of the race, she reinforces the sexual
> instinct, at the risk of disorder, grief and pain. To
> secure strength, she plants cruel hunger and thirst,
> which so easily overdo their office, invite disease.
> But these temporary stays shifts for the protection
> of the young animal shed as fast as they can be
> replaced by nobler sources. We live in youth amidst
> this rabble of passions, quite too tender, quite too
> hungry and irritable. Later, the interiors of mind and
> heart open, and supply grander motives.[2]

Fear, Anger, and Grief

Emerson traced the origin of instinctive feelings to survival adaptations.

> The excess of fear with which the animal frame
> is hedged round, shrinking from cold, starting at
> sight of a snake, or at a sudden noise, protects us,
> through a multitude of groundless alarms, from

---

1   *Conduct of Life,* Power (RWE)
2   *Society and Solitude,* Old Age (RWE)

> some one real danger at last. The lover seeks in
> marriage his private felicity and perfection, with no
> prospective end; and nature hides in his happiness
> her own end, namely, progeny, or the perpetuity of
> the race.[1]

Often, in Shakespeare's plays, characters describe their emotions to the audience. At the beginning of *Macbeth,* kindly King Duncan is murdered. His sons realize that whoever assassinated their father will have them in his sights. Malcolm says to his younger brother,

> This murderous shaft that's shot
> Hath not yet lighted, and our safest way
> Is to avoid the aim.
> Therefore, to horse;
> And let us not be dainty of leave-taking,
> But shift away: there's warrant in that theft
> Which steals itself, when there's no mercy left.[2]

They flee to safety and gather forces that eventually defeat Macbeth.

Shakespeare makes this point about a result of fear.

> In time we hate that which we often fear.[3]

Two fundamental engines of fear are the physical fear of death and the social fear of humiliation. However limited their adherence might be in other respects, people often turn to religion to deny, in death, a permanent yielding of self and separation from their loved ones. Emerson asked his readers to look at this differently.

> The race of mankind have always offered at least
> this implied thanks for the gift of existence, —
> namely, the terror of its being taken away; the
> insatiable curiosity and appetite for its continuation.

---

1   *Essays: Second Series,* Nature (RWE)
2   *Macbeth, Act II,* Scene 3 (WS)
3   *Antony and Cleopatra,* Act I, Scene 3 (WS)

> Of immortality, the soul, when well employed, is
> incurious. It is so well, that it is sure it will be well.
> It asks no questions of the Supreme Power.[1]

The appetite for life's continuation varies according to circumstances. Shakespeare wrote memorable expressions of readiness for death.

> **Hamlet.** O that this too too solid flesh would melt,
> Thaw, and resolve itself into a dew!
> Or that the Everlasting had not fix'd
> His canon 'gainst self-slaughter! O God! God!
> How weary, stale, flat, and unprofitable
> Seem to me all the uses of this world!
> Fie on't! ah, fie![2]

Hamlet regretted God's law against suicide. MacBeth wished an earlier death had spared him emptiness and pain.

> **Macbeth.** Had I but died an hour before this
> chance,
> I had lived a blessed time; for, from this instant,
> There 's nothing serious in mortality:
> All is but toys: renown and grace is dead;
> The wine of life is drawn, and the mere lees
> Is left this vault to brag of.[3]

Later in the play, when informed of his wife's death, Macbeth soliloquized,

> She should have died hereafter;
> There would have been a time for such a word.
> To-morrow, and to-morrow, and to-morrow,
> Creeps in this petty pace from day to day
> To the last syllable of recorded time,
> And all our yesterdays have lighted fools
> The way to dusty death. Out, out, brief candle!

---

1   *Conduct of Life,* Worship (RWE)
2   *Hamlet,* Act I, Scene 2 (WS)
3   *MacBeth,* Act II, Scene 3 (WS)

> Life's but a walking shadow, a poor player
> That struts and frets his hour upon the stage
> And then is heard no more: it is a tale
> Told by an idiot, full of sound and fury,
> Signifying nothing.[1]

Shakespeare stands so high in the pantheon of contributors to world culture because of his remarkable powers of expression. His characters could despair—and they could *rage!* Although we desire peace and tenderness between persons in our real lives, we are ready to be entertained by invective in stories penned by the greats. In *King Lear,* Shakespeare has the Earl of Kent describe his enemy.

> A knave; a rascal; an eater of broken meats;[2]
> a base, proud, shallow, beggarly, three-suited,
> hundred-pound, filthy, worsted-stocking knave; a
> lily-liver'd, action-taking, whoreson, glass-gazing,
> superserviceable, finical rogue; one-trunk-inheriting
> slave; one that wouldst be a bawd in way of good
> service, and art nothing but the composition of a
> knave, beggar, coward, pander, and the son and
> heir of a mongrel bitch; one whom I will beat into
> clamorous whining, if thou deny the least syllable of
> thy addition.[3]

By making his Richard III so thoroughly despicable, Shakespeare sets up the furious speeches of women who have been wronged by him.

> **Richard III.** Have done thy charm, thou hateful
> wither'd hag!
> **Queen Margaret.** And leave out thee? stay, dog, for
> thou shalt hear me.
> If heaven have any grievous plague in store
> Exceeding those that I can wish upon thee,
> O, let them keep it till thy sins be ripe,

---

1   *MacBeth,* Act V, Scene 5 (WS)
2   An "eater of broken meats" is a person who lives off the leavings of others. (WS)
3   *King Lear,* Act II, Scene 2

> And then hurl down their indignation
> On thee, the troubler of the poor world's peace!
> The worm of conscience still begnaw thy soul!
> Thy friends suspect for traitors while thou livest,
> And take deep traitors for thy dearest friends!
> No sleep close up that deadly eye of thine,
> Unless it be whilst some tormenting dream
> Affrights thee with a hell of ugly devils!
> Thou elvish-mark'd, abortive, rooting hog!
> Thou that wast seal'd in thy nativity
> The slave of nature and the son of hell!
> Thou slander of thy mother's heavy womb!
> Thou loathed issue of thy father's loins!
> Thou rag of honour! thou detested—

Speaking about the curses she laid upon her enemy, Queen Margaret warns her friend,

> I'll not believe but they ascend the sky,
> And there awake God's gentle-sleeping peace.
> O Buckingham, take heed of yonder dog!
> Look, when he fawns, he bites; and when he bites,
> His venom tooth will rankle to the death:
> Have not to do with him, beware of him;
> Sin, death, and hell have set their marks on him,
> And all their ministers attend on him.[1]

As with insults, we would rather read about villains, or see them portrayed, than to deal with them in person. The historic Richard III was a mixed bag—but Shakespeare portrayed him onstage as thoroughly evil. Shakespeare's Macbeth was more complicated, more human, but dastardly enough to say,

> False face must hide what the false heart doth know.[2]

In other plays, Shakespeare's characters worry about the effect of anger on their judgment.

---

1 *Richard III*, Act I, Scene 3 (WS)
2 *Macbeth*, Act I, Scene 7 (WS)

> What our contempt doth often hurl from us,
> We wish it ours again; the present pleasure,
> By revolution lowering, does become
> The opposite of itself: she's good, being gone;
> The hand could pluck her back that shoved her on.
> Never anger
> Made good guard for itself.[1]

The American poet Carl Sandburg expressed the same theme.

> Look out how you use proud words.
> When you let proud words go, it is not easy to call
> them back.
> They wear long boots, hard boots; they walk off
> proud; they can't hear you calling -
> Look out how you use proud words.[2]

In some circumstances, angry feelings leave us ashamed of ourselves. In *Othello*, a nasty character uses Cassio's weakness for alcohol against him. Cassio suffers.

> It hath pleased the devil drunkenness to give place
> to the devil wrath; one unperfectness shows me
> another, to make me frankly despise myself.[3]

Parents wish to die before their children. Here's how a Shakespearean father reckons the loss of his son:

> Irreparable is the loss, and patience
> Says it is past her cure.[4]

Madame de Staël mourned the death of her father.

> Unexpectedly, at a time when I felt completely free
> from apprehension, I found two letters on my table,
> telling me that my father was dangerously ill. I was
> not informed that the courier who had brought

---

1   *Antony and Cleopatra,* Act IV, Scene 1 (WS)
2   *Primer Lessons,* Carl Sandburg
3   *Othello,* Act II, Scene 3 (WS)
4   *The Tempest,* Act V, Scene 1 (WS)

them had also brought the news of his death. I set
out with hope, which I retained in spite of all the
circumstances that should have extinguished it.
At Weimar, when the truth was revealed to me, I
was seized by a feeling of inexpressible terror and
despair. I saw myself with no support in the world,
compelled to face misfortune all by myself. There
was still much in life to interest me, but the loving
admiration I had felt for my father exercised an
influence over me that nothing else could equal.
—the truest of prophets-made me realize that
henceforth I should never be as completely
happy as I had been as long as this exceedingly
compassionate man watched over my fate, and
not a single day has passed —since the month
of April, 1804—in which I have not connected all
my sorrows with his loss. While my father lived
I suffered only through my imagination, for with
real problems he always found a way to help me.
After losing him, I had to deal directly with destiny.
However, I owe what strength I still have to the
hope that he is praying for me in heaven. It is not
filial love, but intimate knowledge of his character
which makes me affirm that I have never seen
human nature closer to perfection than in him; if I
were not convinced of a future life, I would go mad
at the idea that such a being could have ceased to
exist. There was such a sense of immortality about
his feelings and thoughts that very often when
I experience unusually exalted emotions I can
believe that I am hearing him still.
During my sad journey from Weimar to Coppet I
felt envious of all the life that was stirring in nature,
even the birds and insects flying around me.[1]

The word "I" appears over and over; she grieves the
loss to herself— a valuable resource is hers no more. When
she pictures her father in heaven, she hopes he is *praying for
her*—still sending care her way. We cannot fault her—everyone
is centered in self; that is how we are made. Our feelings stem

---

1   *Ten Years of Exile,* Madame de Staël

from our needs and our thoughts are bent on getting them filled and keeping them topped off.

We regard sympathy as a positive feeling, but how would we fare, in reading the daily news, if our sympathy flowed unchecked? Emerson advised,

> Regret calamities, if you can thereby help the
> sufferer; if not, attend your own work, and already
> the evil begins to be repaired.[1]

Here's an echo from Shakespeare:

> Care is no cure, but rather corrosive,
> For things that are not to be remedied.[2]

There is much to wring our hands about in the big world. In the small worlds in which our individual effects can be felt, focusing on our own concerns can make life better for those around us.

> Presently, a new experience gives a new turn to
> our thoughts: common sense resumes its tyranny:
> we say, — on the whole, selfishness plants best,
> prunes best, makes the best commerce, and
> the best citizen. ... Does the general voice of
> ages affirm any principle, or is no community of
> sentiment discoverable in distant times and places?
> And when it shows the power of self-interest, I
> accept that as part of the divine law, and must
> reconcile it with aspiration the best I can.[3]

Moods

Madame de Staël was conscious of her shifting moods.

> I am by nature very impressionable; my imagination
> more readily turns to pain than hope, and although
> I have often found that my sorrow is dissipated by a
> new set of circumstances, at first I am always sure

1   *Essays,* Self Reliance (RWE)
2   *Henry VI Part 1,* Act III, Scene 3 (WS)
3   *Representative Men,* Montaigne; or, the Skeptic (RWE)

that nothing can rescue me from it. It is so easy to be
unhappy, especially for those who set their sights on
life's finer prizes.[1]

Shakespeare's characters have moods. In *The Tempest,* after
a crabby-sounding outburst from her father, Miranda tries to
reassure her young man.

> Be of comfort;
> My father's of a better nature, sir,
> Than he appears by speech: this is unwonted
> Which now came from him.[2]

Brutus apologized for his ill-humors.

> Vexed I am
> Of late with passions of some difference,
> Conceptions only proper to myself,
> Which give some soil perhaps to my behaviors;
> But let not therefore my good friends be grieved—
> Among which number, Cassius, be you one—
> Nor construe any further my neglect,
> Than that poor Brutus, with himself at war,
> Forgets the shows of love to other men.[3]

Emerson gave us images for moodiness.

> Life is a train of moods like a string of beads, and,
> as we pass through them, they prove to be many-
> colored lenses which paint the world their own hue,
> and each shows only what lies in its focus. From the
> mountain you see the mountain. We animate what we
> can, and we see only what we animate. Nature and
> books belong to the eyes that see them. It depends
> on the mood of the man, whether he shall see the
> sunset or the fine poem. There are always sunsets,
> and there is always genius; but only a few hours so
> serene that we can relish nature or criticism.[4]

---

1   *Ten Years of Exile,* Madame de Staël
2   *The Tempest,* Act I, Scene 2 (WS)
3   *Julius Caesar,* Act I, Scene 2 (WS)
4   *Essays: Second Series,* Temperament (RWE)

> Our life is March weather, savage and serene in one hour.[1]

> The secret of the illusoriness is in the necessity of a succession of moods or objects. Gladly we would anchor, but the anchorage is quicksand. This onward trick of nature is too strong for us.[2]

> Our moods do not believe in each other. Today, I am full of thoughts, and can write what I please. I see no reason why I should not have the same thought, the same power of expression tomorrow. What I write, whilst I write it, seems the most natural thing in the world: but, yesterday, I saw a dreary vacuity in this direction in which now I see so much; and a month hence, I doubt not, I shall wonder who he was that wrote so many continuous pages. Alas for this infirm faith, this will not strenuous, this vast ebb of a vast flow! I am God in nature; I am a weed by the wall.[3]

Sometimes Emerson wrote directly from his own experience. He confesses,

> If we were not of all opinions! if we did not in any moment shift the platform on which we stand, and look and speak from another! if there could be any regulation, any 'one-hour-rule,' that a man should never leave his point of view, without sound of trumpet. I am always insincere, as always knowing there are other moods.[4]

Our insecure feelings affect our moods.

> Each man sees his own life defaced and disfigured, as the life of man is not, to his imagination. Each man sees over his own experience a certain slime of error, whilst that of other men looks fair and ideal.[5]

---

1   *Representative Men,* Montaigne; or, the Skeptic (RWE)
2   *Essays: Second Series,* Experience (RWE)
3   *Essays,* Circles (RWE)
4   *Essays: Second Series,* Nominalist and Realist (RWE)
5   *Essays,* Love (RWE)

Anxieties are a constant distraction.

> An old French verse runs, in my translation:
>   Some of your griefs you have cured,
>   And the sharpest you still have survived;
>   But what torments of pain you endured
>   From evils that never arrived![1]

How excellent is that "old French verse"?

At some point our ability to think critically, which we cultivate, can become a sour attitude—pointless and destructive.

> I cannot afford to be irritable and captious, nor to waste all my time in attacks. If I should go out of church whenever I hear a false sentiment, I could never stay there five minutes. But why come out? The street is as false as the church, and when I get to my house, or to my manners, or to my speech, I have not got away from the lie.[2]

Emerson wanted us to lighten up.

> We must pay for being too intellectual, as they call it. People are not as light-hearted for it. I think men never loved life less. I question if care and doubt ever wrote their names so legibly on the faces of any population. This *ennui*, for which we Saxons had no name, this word of France has got a terrific significance. It shortens life, and bereaves the day of its light.[3]

One form of irritability is a propensity for boredom. Because the acuity of Madame de Staël's tongue and pen was anathema to Napoleon, he exiled her. Her *ennui* was increased by her exclusion from Paris, but reduced by her fascination with his skill in wielding power.

---

1   *Conduct of Life*, Considerations by the Way (RWE)
2   *Essays: Second Series*, New England Reformers (RWE)
3   *Addresses*, Lecture on the Times (RWE)

> The specter of boredom has always pursued me;
> because of my terror of it, I might have yielded
> to tyranny if the example of my father, and his
> blood that flows in my veins, had not enabled me
> to triumph over this weakness. Be that as it may,
> Bonaparte knew this foible of mine very well. He
> is quick to discern a person's weak points, for it is
> through their flaws that he subjugates people.
>
> To the power with which he threatens and the
> treasures with which he entices, he adds relief from
> boredom: always anathema to a Frenchman.[1]

Emerson thought that an innately positive outlook was greatest good fortune.

> In the scale of powers, it is not talent, but
> sensibility, which is best: talent confines, but the
> central life puts us in relation to all. How often it
> seems the chief good to be born with a cheerful
> temper, and well adjusted to the tone of the human
> race. Such a man feels himself in harmony, and
> conscious by his receptivity of an infinite strength.[2]

We should try to view the world through a sunny lens, and not press too hard with our intellects.

> The world is enigmatical, — everything said, and
> everything known or done, — and must not be
> taken literally, but genially. We must be at the top
> of our condition to understand anything rightly.
> You must hear the bird's song without attempting
> to render it into nouns and verbs. Cannot we be a
> little abstemious and obedient? Cannot we let the
> morning be?[3]

That second sentence makes this a difficult paragraph to understand. I think that he meant *we are at the top of our condition* when we can relax our nearly irresistible verbal

---

1   *Ten Years of Exile,* Madame de Staël
2   *Society and Solitude,* Success (RWE)
3   *Society and Solitude,* Works and Days (RWE)

impulses and *understand things rightly* by allowing ourselves pure sensory experience of the world around us.

> Ah! if one could keep this sensibility, and live in the happy sufficing present, and find the day and its cheap means contenting, which only ask receptivity in you, and no strained exertion and cankering ambition, overstimulating to be at the head of your class and the head of society, and to have distinction and laurels and consumption! We are not strong by our power to penetrate, but by our relatedness. The world is enlarged for us, not by new objects, but by finding more affinities and potencies in those we have.[1]

Hope and Happiness

People have personal hopes, and hopes for loved ones, and hopes for mankind. That last hope can seem forlorn. Emerson acknowledged that the past has been dismal, but clung to his optimism:

> The argument, which is always forthcoming to silence those who conceive extraordinary hopes of man, namely, the appeal to experience, is forever invalid and vain. A mightier hope abolishes despair. We give up the past to the objector, and yet we hope.[2]

Whitman wrote of hope.

> As sitting in dark days,
> Lone, sulky, through the time's thick murk looking in vain for light, for hope,
> From unsuspected parts a fierce and momentary proof,
> (The sun there at the centre though conceal'd,
> Electric life forever at the centre,)
> Breaks forth a lightning flash.[3]

> Now trumpeter for thy close,
> Vouchsafe a higher strain than any yet,

---

1 *Society and Solitude,* Success (RWE)
2 *Essays,* The Oversoul (RWE)
3 *Leaves of Grass,* Far from Dakota's Canyons (WW)

> Sing to my soul, renew its languishing faith and
> hope,
> Rouse up my slow belief, give me some vision of
> the future,
> Give me for once its prophecy and joy.[1]

And from Emerson,

> Life is an ecstasy. Life is sweet as nitrous oxide; and
> the fisherman dripping all day over a cold pond, the
> switchman at the railway intersection, the farmer
> in the field, the negro in the rice-swamp, the fop
> in the street, the hunter in the woods, the barrister
> with the jury, the belle at the ball, all ascribe a
> certain pleasure to their employment, which they
> themselves give it. Health and appetite impart the
> sweetness to sugar, bread, and meat.[2]

Apparently Emerson's dentist used nitrous oxide to temper
pain and anxiety.

We use the word *happiness* in at least two senses. One form
of happiness comes in bursts, as when a child runs to you
with outspread arms. The other refers to a cumulative state—
contentment at the terms of your life.

> Hume's[3] doctrine was that the circumstances vary,
> the amount of happiness does not; that the beggar
> cracking fleas in the sunshine under a hedge, and
> the duke rolling by in his chariot, the girl equipped
> for her first ball, and the orator returning triumphant
> from the debate, had different means, but the same
> quantity of pleasant excitement.[4]

> To fill the hour, — that is happiness; to fill the
> hour, and leave no crevice for a repentance or an
> approval. We live amid surfaces, and the true art of
> life is to skate well on them.[5]

---

1 *Leaves of Grass,* The Mystic Trumpeter (WW)
2 *Conduct of Life,* Illusions (RWE)
3 David Hume (1711-1776) was a Scottish philosopher of the
  Enlightenment era.
4 *Society and Solitude,* Works and Days (RWE)
5 *Essays: Second Series,* Experience (RWE)

It is said of Emerson that a disproportionate share of his sentences are topic sentences—that his style is highly aphoristic. The two sentences above are an example. Both of them provoke thought, but it's not clear how the second follows the first. The challenge to live our days without self-reproach or striving to notch approval—isn't that an excellent aim? Difficult for me, but, truly, our reach should exceed our grasp. Next comes another thought—*we live amid surfaces.* Spouse, job, parents and perhaps offspring, a dwelling, a circle of friends, a community, a hobby or two, and whatever media we see or hear—are these what he means by the surfaces we live amongst? Skating smoothly from one to another, keeping your balance—I could accept that as an image for the art of living.

Elsewhere Emerson quotes Macbeth's summary of the good things his evil behavior had denied him.

> A cultivated person fitly surrounded by a happy home, "with honor, love, obedience, troops of friends," is of all institutions the best.[1]

Love

Above, under Courtship, we have heard something from our authors about love. They have more to say—of all feelings, love has the best publicity agents. Shakespeare was in their pocket. In *The Tempest,* the protagonist-father is pleased by the speedy growth of love between his daughter and a handsome prince.

> **Prospero.** Fair encounter
> Of two most rare affections! Heavens rain grace
> On that which breeds between 'em![2]

---

1 *English Traits,* Personal (RWE)
2 *The Tempest,* Act III, Scene 1 (WS)

The prologue of *Romeo and Juliet* summarizes the tragic plot, in which teenagers from feuding families fall for each other.

> **Chorus.** Two households, both alike in dignity,
> In fair Verona, where we lay our scene,
> From ancient grudge break to new mutiny,
> Where civil blood makes civil hands unclean.
> From forth the fatal loins of these two foes
> A pair of star-cross'd lovers take their life;
> Whose misadventured piteous overthrows
> Do with their death bury their parents' strife.
> The fearful passage of their death-mark'd love,
> And the continuance of their parents' rage,
> Which, but their children's end, nought could remove,
> Is now the two hours' traffic of our stage;
> The which if you with patient ears attend,
> What here shall miss, our toil shall strive to mend.

In the first act, Romeo, who had thought he was in love with a different girl, first sees Juliet.

> **Romeo.** O, she doth teach the torches to burn bright!
> It seems she hangs upon the cheek of night
> Like a rich jewel in an Ethiope's ear;
> Beauty too rich for use, for earth too dear!
> So shows a snowy dove trooping with crows,
> As yonder lady o'er her fellows shows.
> The measure done, I'll watch her place of stand,
> And, touching hers, make blessed my rude hand.
> Did my heart love till now? forswear it, sight!
> For I ne'er saw true beauty till this night.[1]

At the end of the scene we learn that Juliet reciprocates Romeo's first-sight passion. She is soon to learn that he is one of her family's enemies.

---

1   *Romeo and Juliet,* Act I Scene 5 (WS)

> **Juliet.** My only love sprung from my only hate!
> Too early seen unknown, and known too late!
> Prodigious birth of love it is to me,
> That I must love a loathed enemy.

In the next act, Romeo tells a friendly priest of his heart's rapid change of love objects. The priest reflects on the nature of such transitory love.

> Is Rosaline, whom thou didst love so dear,
> So soon forsaken? young men's love then lies
> Not truly in their hearts, but in their eyes.[1]

The strength of this teenage crush drives the action of the play. The word love is used 175 times, despite the repeated admission that this form of love is attractive youth lusting after attractive youth, with no opportunity to test the potential for companionship. The continued appeal of *Romeo and Juliet* (retold in the last century as *West Side Story*) attests to our fascination with this high-voltage feeling. Emerson saw it.

> For, though the celestial rapture falling out of
> heaven seizes only upon those of tender age, and
> although a beauty overpowering all analysis or
> comparison, and putting us quite beside ourselves,
> we can seldom see after thirty years, yet the
> remembrance of these visions outlasts all other
> remembrances, and is a wreath of flowers on the
> oldest brows.[2]

Whitman did not neglect this theme.

> Blow again trumpeter! and for thy theme,
>   Take now the enclosing theme of all, the solvent
> and the setting,
>   Love, that is pulse of all, the sustenance and the
> pang,
>   The heart of man and woman all for love,

---

1 *Romeo and Juliet*, Act II Scene 3 (WS)
2 *Essays*, Love (RWE)

No other theme but love—knitting, enclosing, all-diffusing love.[1]

"They say that breaking up is hard to do; Now I know, I know that it's true," played on rock and roll radio a million times when I was young. Emerson mentioned love's complications.

> In the noon and the afternoon of life, we still throb at the recollection of days when happiness was not happy enough, but must be drugged with the relish of pain and fear; for he touched the secret of the matter, who said of love, "All other pleasures are not worth its pains;" and when the day was not long enough, but the night too must be consumed in keen recollections.[2]

Madame de Staël wrote that love, prominent in Shakespeare and other Elizabethan drama, was absent from Greek drama. She explained,

> All men have undoubtedly known mental anguish, and its forceful description in Homer is acknowledged. But the power to love seems to have grown with other advances of the human mind and, above all, through the new customs that summoned women to share life with men. Shameless prostitutes, slaves degraded by their fate, women secluded in their homes and unknown to the rest of the world, strangers to the concerns of their husbands, reared to have neither ideas nor feelings—this is all the Greeks knew of the ties of love.[3]

We can't choose our feelings but we can choose what to do about them. Any resource that helps us build character does so in part because it helps us manage our emotions.

---

1 *Leaves of Grass,* The Mystic Trumpeter (WW)
2 *Essays,* Love (RWE)
3 *Ten Years of Exile,* Madame de Staël

Resources

The work of our lives is the unfolding of self in the direction that calls us. It is challenging work. Obstacles frequently bar the way. Limitations of circumstance can defy penetration. Distractions are plentiful. Fortunately, we are not without resources.

Language

For human beings, language is the fundamental resource. Facility at receiving and sending language lends power. An articulate person himself, Emerson tipped his hat to an Englishman.

> Shakespeare's principal merit may be conveyed, in saying that he, of all men, best understands the English language, and can say what he will.[1]

> Children cry, scream, and stamp with fury, unable to express their desires. As soon as they can speak and tell their want, and the reason of it, they become gentle. In adult life, whilst the perceptions are obtuse, men and women talk vehemently and superlatively, blunder and quarrel: their manners are full of desperation; their speech is full of oaths. As soon as, with culture, things have cleared up a little, and they see them no longer in lumps and masses, but accurately distributed, they desist from that weak vehemence, and explain their meaning in detail. If the tongue had not been framed for articulation, man would still be a beast in the forest.[2]

> The same weakness and want, on a higher plane, occurs daily in the education of ardent young men and women. 'Ah! you don't understand me; I have never met with any one who comprehends me,' and they sigh and weep, write verses, and walk alone, — fault of power to express their precise meaning.

---

1 *Representative Men*, Uses of Great Men (RWE)
2 *Representative Men*, Plato; or, the Philosopher (RWE)

> In a month or two, through the favor of their good
> genius, they meet some one so related as to assist
> their volcanic estate; and, good communication
> being once established, they are thenceforward
> good citizens. It is ever thus. The progress is to
> accuracy, to skill, to truth, from blind force.[1]

When modern parents remind a young child to "Use your words" they are acting on Emerson's belief that our attitudes and behavior improve with our ability to express ourselves.

> The basis of poetry is language, which is material
> only on one side. It is a demi-god.[2]

A demi-god is the offspring of a divinity and a human being. Hercules, for example, was the son of Zeus and Alcmene, a mortal woman. By comparing language to a demi-god, Emerson brings to mind the last stage of human evolution. Primitive hunters who could use language to plan and coordinate were most productive, and as warriors, most victorious. The capacity for practical communication spiraled upwards until the language of Shakespeare and Emerson developed. Language was not a gift of the gods. Language enabled human beings to create their gods. "In the beginning was the Word . . ."

Do you write? In *Leaves of Grass,* Walt Whitman offers encouragement.

> Whoever you are! claim your own at any hazard!
>   These shows of the East and West are tame
> compared to you,
>   These immense meadows, these interminable
> rivers, you are immense
>   and interminable as they,
>   These furies, elements, storms, motions of Nature,
> throes of apparent

---

1 *Representative Men,* Plato; or, the Philosopher (RWE)
2 *Society and Solitude,* Art (RWE)

    dissolution, you are he or she who is master or
mistress over them,
  Master or mistress in your own right over Nature,
elements, pain,
    passion, dissolution.

  The hopples fall from your ankles, you find an
unfailing sufficiency,
  Old or young, male or female, rude, low, rejected by
the rest,
    whatever you are promulges itself,
  Through birth, life, death, burial, the means are
provided, nothing
    is scanted,
  Through angers, losses, ambition, ignorance, ennui,
what you are
    picks its way.[1]

Here's Whitman on the joys of self-expression:

The spotted hawk swoops by and accuses me, he
complains of my gab
    and my loitering.
  I too am not a bit tamed, I too am untranslatable,
  I sound my barbaric yawp over the roofs of the world.
  The last scud of day holds back for me,
  It flings my likeness after the rest and true as any on
the shadow'd wilds,
  It coaxes me to the vapor and the dusk.
  I depart as air, I shake my white locks at the runaway
sun,
  I effuse my flesh in eddies, and drift it in lacy jags.
  I bequeath myself to the dirt to grow from the grass I
love,
  If you want me again look for me under your boot-
soles.
  You will hardly know who I am or what I mean,
  But I shall be good health to you nevertheless,
  And filter and fibre your blood.

---

1 *Leaves of Grass,* You (WW)

> Failing to fetch me at first keep encouraged,
> Missing me one place search another,
> I stop somewhere waiting for you.[1]

Emerson had advice for writers.

> The way to speak and write what shall not go out
> of fashion, is, to speak and write sincerely. The
> argument which has not power to reach my own
> practice, I may well doubt, will fail to reach yours.
> But take Sidney's[2] maxim: "Look in thy heart, and
> write." He that writes to himself, writes to an eternal
> public. That statement only is fit to be made public
> which you have come at in attempting to satisfy
> your own curiosity.[3]

Intelligence and Creativity

The intellect is a resource of the first importance, because,

> The intellect goes out of the individual, floats over
> its own personality, and regards it as a fact, and
> not as I and mine. He who is immersed in what
> concerns person or place, cannot see the problem
> of existence. This the intellect always ponders.[4]

The first sentence refers to the capacity for self-awareness, without which we are hamstrung in our efforts to sculpt ourselves. The second two sentences go a different direction, to the matter of thought. Everyone needn't contemplate the problem of existence, which, after all, is an unsolvable mystery. But people who engage that mystery are more apt to see things from multiple points of view—their pondering leads them on, which makes them better company and rewarding friends.

> As with events, so is it with thoughts. When I watch
> that flowing river, which, out of regions I see not,

---

1   *Leaves of Grass,* Song of Myself (WW)
2   Sir Philip Sidney (1554-1586) was a literary light in
    Elizabethan England.
3   *Essays,* Spiritual Laws (RWE)
4   *Essays,* Intellect (RWE)

> pours for a season its streams into me, I see that
> I am a pensioner, not a cause, but a surprised
> spectator of this ethereal water; that I desire and
> look up, and put myself in the attitude of reception,
> but from some alien energy the visions come.[1]

This sounds mystical at first reading, but I think the experience is common to all who create things—not just poems or paintings but also flower arrangements and cooking and woodworking, when you watch your hands seem to do things on their own. In this "attitude of reception," whether the source of the flow is your prior experience or some pre-conscious capacity, the conscious self can indeed feel like a spectator.

Alternatively, the intellect stays in the driver's seat and analyzes the situation, attempting to solve problems by identifying chains of cause and effect.

> The progress of the intellect consists in the
> clearer vision of causes, which overlooks surface
> differences.[2]

> Thought dissolves the material universe, by carrying
> the mind up into a sphere where all is plastic.[3]

The ability to recognize patterns is a critical mental resource. We use the word *penetration* when intelligence perceives underlying patterns, undeceived by superficial differences.

> What is the hardest task in the world? To think.
> I would put myself in the attitude to look in the
> eye an abstract truth, and I cannot. ... Then, in a
> moment, and unannounced, the truth appears.
> A certain, wandering light appears, and is the
> distinction, the principle we wanted. But the oracle
> comes, because we had previously laid siege to

---

1   *Essays,* The Over-soul (RWE)
2   *Essays,* History (RWE)
3   *Conduct of Life,* Fate (RWE)

the shrine. It seems as if the law of the intellect resembled that law of nature by which we now inspire, now expire the breath; by which the heart now draws in, then hurls out the blood, the law of undulation. So now you must labor with your brains, and now you must forbear your activity, and see what the great Soul showeth.[1]

Margaret Fuller sounded a similar note.

Let us be wise, and not impede the soul. Let her work as she will. Let us have one creative energy, one incessant revelation. Let it take what form it will, and let us not bind it by the past to man or woman, black or white.[2]

This usage of the word soul by both writers is provocative. Is the *great Soul* an immanent divinity to which we ought to tune in? Is that the same soul that Fuller doesn't want us to impede? Or is she referring to a core self, our deepest font of understanding? Does either Emerson or Fuller believe in a creative force apart from nature and humanity? Or do they use religious terminology because they are trying to give spiritual counsel, and this is the vocabulary of that undertaking?

After the work of thought has been performed, and you have reached a conclusion provisionally satisfactory to yourself, you might dare to discuss it, exposing your idea to challenge or contradiction. Emerson offered a test for this situation.

Why should I give up my thought, because I cannot answer an objection to it? Consider only, whether it remains in my life the same [as] it was.[3]

You can hear the arguments against your idea and file them for future reference, but if your idea continues to ring true to you, there is no need to give it up. You might adopt another notion as an alternative way of looking at the matter, or not. The

1 *Essays,* Intellect (RWE)
2 *Woman in the Nineteenth Century,* Margaret Fuller
3 *Conduct of Life,* Worship (RWE)

point is that you don't have to rush to reject either proposition. You can wait and see which best bears wear in your mental life.

Perhaps Emerson is speaking from personal experience when he wrote the following:

> The direct splendor of intellectual power is ever welcome in fine society as the costliest addition to its rule and its credit.
> The dry light must shine in to adorn our festival, but it must be tempered and shaded, or that will also offend. Accuracy is essential to beauty, and quick perceptions to politeness, but not too quick perceptions. One may be too punctual and too precise.[1]

You might be the smartest person in the room but it is a social error to be caught proving it. And yet, as Emerson noted, your companions respect your intelligence and want the benefit of it.

Emerson admonished us to trust our own intellectual stars, but later in his life he played down originality.

> Great men are more distinguished by range and extent, than by originality. If we require the originality which consists in weaving, like a spider, their web from their own bowels; in finding clay, and making bricks, and building the house; no great men are original. Nor does valuable originality consist in unlikeness to other men.[2]

The great man he is talking about here is Shakespeare, who borrowed plots and themes from literature and tradition and recast them into plays that have proven timeless. Their staying power stems from their capture of human traits, thoughts, and feelings. Shakespeare didn't make these up. *Original* is a slippery designation. Emerson (and many others) ranked Shakespeare as the supreme master of the reshuffling of the elements of

---

1 *Essays: Second Series,* Manners (RWE)
2 *Representative Men,* Shakespeare; or the Poet (RWE)

experience to illuminate human nature. Emerson saluted the bard,

> The Imagination may be defined to be, the use
> which the Reason makes of the material world.
> Shakespeare possesses the power of subordinating
> nature for the purposes of expression, beyond all
> poets. His imperial muse tosses the creation like a
> bauble from hand to hand, and uses it to embody
> any caprice of thought that is upper-most in his
> mind. The remotest spaces of nature are visited,
> and the farthest sundered things are brought
> together, by a subtle spiritual connection.[1]

In this context Emerson used *nature* to mean everything outside the mind.

His sense of *muse* corresponds to Margaret Fuller's definition.

> What I mean by the Muse is that unimpeded
> clearness of the intuitive powers, which a perfectly
> truthful adherence to every admonition of the higher
> instincts would bring to a finely organized human
> being.[2]

Unimpeded clearness of the intuitive powers implies a free flow of imagination. Emerson recalled,

> There are no days in life so memorable as those
> which vibrated to some stroke of the imagination.[3]

That is true for me. I can picture the moment in my Chicago apartment that I thought of using peanuts in tabletop animations. Their comical resemblance to human figures opened the door to my first occupation: making films for children. Because my animations used peanuts as people, forks as wild animals, and shaving brushes as dolphins, it struck me to find, so much later in life, this line in Emerson:

---

1 *Nature,* Idealism (RWE)
2 *Woman in the Nineteenth Century,* Margaret Fuller
3 *Conduct of Life,* Beauty (RWE)

> The feat of the imagination is in showing the
> convertibility of everything into every other thing.[1]

The resource of our intelligence is at its best when based on our whole experience, which feels like spontaneous intuition. Later we can devise logical defenses if we need to. Emerson wrote,

> Our spontaneous action is always the best. You
> cannot, with your best deliberation and heed, come
> so close to any question as your spontaneous glance
> shall bring you, whilst you rise from your bed, or walk
> abroad in the morning after meditating the matter
> before sleep, on the previous night.[2]

Innovators like Franklin and Edison deflected references to their genius with allusions to the greater role of concentrated effort in attainment of their success. Emerson made the same point, quoting an artist.

> "Ah!" said a brave painter to me, "if a man has failed,
> you will find he has dreamed instead of working.
> There is no way to success in our art, but to take off
> your coat, grind paint, and work like a digger on the
> railroad, all day and every day."
>
> … The one prudence in life is concentration; the one
> evil is dissipation: and it makes no difference whether
> our dissipations are coarse or fine; property and its
> cares, friends, and a social habit, or politics, or music,
> or feasting. Everything is good which takes away one
> plaything and delusion more, and drives us home
> to add one stroke of faithful work. Friends, books,
> pictures, lower duties, talents, flatteries, hopes, — all
> are distractions which cause oscillations in our giddy
> balloon and make a good poise and a straight course
> impossible. You must elect your work; you shall take
> what your brain can, and drop all the rest.[3]

---

1   *Conduct of Life,* Beauty (RWE)
2   *Essays,* Intellect (RWE)
3   *Conduct of Life,* Power (RWE)

This is exaggerated to emphasize the cost of distractions. Living a balanced life in family and community, and having friends, requires you to look up from your work. Emerson did.

Culture

High among the resources for personhood are reading and books. Good books offer the pleasure of well-wrought sentences and paragraphs and an enormous variety of information. Books provoke intellectual activity.

> What can we see or acquire, but what we are? You have seen a skilful man reading Virgil. Well, that author is a thousand books to a thousand persons. Take the book into your two hands, and read your eyes out; you will never find what I find.[1]

> There is then creative reading as well as creative writing. When the mind is braced by labor and invention, the page of whatever book we read becomes luminous with manifold allusion.[2]

> The joyful reader borrows of his own ideas to fill their faulty outline, and knows not that he borrows and gives.[3]

> As no air-pump can by any means make a perfect vacuum, so neither can any artist entirely exclude the conventional, the local, the perishable from his book or write a book of pure thought, that shall be as efficient, in respects to a remote posterity, as to contemporaries, or rather to the second age. Each age, it is found, must write its own books; or rather, each generation for the next succeeding. The books of an older period will not fit this.[4]

---

1   *Essays,* Spiritual Laws (RWE)
2   *Addresses,* The American Scholar (RWE)
3   *Society and Solitude,* Success (RWE)
4   *Addresses,* The American Scholar (RWE)

Thus said Emerson to himself, in his humility, and it has much truth, although his thought remains worthy of attention. His opening sentence in the following, for example, lists of hazards for a book of thought, with respect to its shelf life. He made this remark in an early lecture, in 1837, in which he went on to state the limited value, to a given learner, of any one book.

> The books which once we valued more than the apple of the eye, we have quite exhausted. What is that but saying, that we have come up with the point of view which the universal mind took through the eyes of one scribe; we have been that man, and have passed on. First, one; then, another; we drain all cisterns, and, waxing greater by all these supplies, we crave a better and more abundant food. The man has never lived that can feed us ever.[1]

> Books are the best of things, well used; abused, among the worst. What is the right use? What is the one end, which all means go to effect? They are for nothing but to inspire. I had better never see a book, than to be warped by its attraction clean out of my own orbit, and made a satellite instead of a system. The one thing in the world, of value, is the active soul.[2]

In a later essay entitled "Books," Emerson wrote,

> ... there are books which ... take rank in our life with parents and lovers and passionate experiences, so medicinal, so stringent, so revolutionary, so authoritative— ... Consider what you have in the smallest chosen library. A company of the wisest and wittiest men that could be picked out of all civil countries, in a thousand years, have set in best order the results of their learning and wisdom.[3]

---

1   *Addresses,* The American Scholar (RWE)
2   *Addresses,* The American Scholar (RWE)
3   *Society and Solitude,* Books (RWE)

Emerson had mixed feelings about works of fiction.

> Nature has a magic by which she fits the man to his fortunes, by making them the fruit of his character. But the novelist plucks this event here, and that fortune there, and ties them rashly to his figures, to tickle the fancy of his readers with a cloying success, or scare them with shocks of tragedy. And so, on the whole, 'tis a juggle. We are cheated into laughter or wonder by feats which only oddly combine acts that we do every day. There is no new element, no power, no furtherance. 'Tis only confectionery, not the raising of new corn. Great is the poverty of their inventions. She was beautiful and he fell in love.[1]

But, on the other hand,

> Indeed, when one observes how ill and ugly people make their loves and quarrels, 't is pity they should not read novels a little more, to import the fine generosities, and the clear, firm conduct, which are as becoming in the unions and separations which love effects under shingle roofs as in palaces and among illustrious personages.[2]

Emerson was willing to give novelists that much credit—but his highest accolade was *poet*.

> The poet is the person in whom the powers are in balance, the man without impediment, who sees and handles that which others dream of, traverses the whole scale of experience, and is representative of man, in virtue of being the largest power to receive and to impart.[3]

Whitman also praised poets and their powers.

---

1   *Society and Solitude,* Books (RWE)
2   *Society and Solitude,* Books (RWE)
3   *Essays: Second Series,* The Poet (RWE)

The words of the singers are the hours or minutes
of the light or dark,
  but the words of the maker of poems are the
general light and dark,
  The maker of poems settles justice, reality,
immortality,
  His insight and power encircle things and the
human race,
  He is the glory and extract thus far of things and
of the human race.[1]

The poet Emerson most admired was Shakespeare.

Shakespeare read the hearts of men and women,
their probity, and their second thought,and wiles;
the wiles of innocence, and the transitions by
which virtues and vices slide into their contraries.
All the sweets and all the terrors of human lot lay in
his mind as truly but as softly as the landscape lies
on the eye. He is inconceivably wise.
He is wise without emphasis or assertion; he is
strong, as nature is strong, who lifts the land into
mountain slopes without effort, and by the same
rule as she floats a bubble in the air, and likes as
well to do the one as the other. This makes that
equality of power in farce, tragedy, narrative, and
love-songs a merit so incessant, that each reader
is incredulous of the perception of other readers.[2]

In sad contrast to Shakespeare come the rest of us.

I know not how it is that we need an interpreter;
but the great majority of men seem to be minors,
who have not yet come into possession of their
own, or mutes, who cannot report the conversation
they have had with nature.[3]

Emerson identified this difficulty with the resource of
books:

1　*Leaves of Grass,* Song of the Answerer (WW)
2　*Representative Men,* Shakespeare; or, the Poet (RWE)
3　*Essays: Second Series,* The Poet (RWE)

The number of printed books extant today may
easily exceed a million. It is easy to count the
number of pages which a diligent man can read in
a day, and the number of years which human life
in favorable circumstances allows to reading; and
to demonstrate, that, though he should read from
dawn till dark, for sixty years, he must die in the first
alcoves.[1]

The problem of the multiplicity of books, the volume of
volumes, has become far worse. Here is Emerson's advice:

The three practical rules, then, which I have to offer,
are, — 1. Never read any book that is not a year old.
2. Never read any but famed books. 3. Never read
any but what you like; or, in Shakespeare's phrase,
"No profit goes where is no pleasure ta'en: In brief,
sir, study what you most affect."[2]

Read books that you want to discuss with your friends, or
that they want to discuss with you, or that give you pleasure or
broaden your understanding.

The search for meaning has periodically led me to the
weighty literature of philosophy. Shakespeare had some fun
with that impulse.

Touchstone. Hast any philosophy in thee,
shepherd?
Corin. No more but that I know the more one
sickens the worse at ease he is; and that he that
wants money, means, and content, is without three
good friends; that the property of rain is to wet, and
fire to burn; that good pasture makes fat sheep; and
that a great cause of the night is lack of the sun;
that he that hath learned no wit by nature nor art
may complain of good breeding, or comes of a very
dull kindred.
Touchstone. Such a one is a natural philosopher.[3]

---

1 *Society and Solitude,* Books (RWE)
2 *Society and Solitude,* Books (RWE)
3 *As You Like It,* Act III, Scene 2 (WS)

> **Leonato.** I pray thee, peace. I will be flesh and
> blood;
> For there was never yet philosopher
> That could endure the toothache patiently.[1]

Emerson was always philosophic but he was not a professional philosopher. He produced no system of thought. Madame de Staël remarked,

> I have been asked how I would define the word
> philosophy. I understand by philosophy the general
> knowledge of cause and effect in the human realm
> or in physical nature, the freedom of the mind, the
> exercise of thought—in short, in literature those
> works that result from reflection or analysis and
> that are not merely the product of the imagination,
> the emotions, or the feelings.[2]

Philosophy is a resource to the extent that it helps you comprehend your circumstances.

> The Bacon, the Spinoza, the Hume, Schelling,
> Kant, or whosoever propounds to you a philosophy
> of the mind, is only a more or less awkward
> translator of things in your consciousness, which
> you have also your way of seeing, perhaps of
> denominating. Say then, instead of too timidly
> poring into his obscure sense, that he has
> not succeeded in rendering back to you your
> consciousness. He has not succeeded; now let
> another try. If Plato cannot, perhaps Spinoza will. If
> Spinoza cannot, then perhaps Kant.[3]

> No power of genius has ever yet had the smallest
> success in explaining existence.[4]

---

1   *Much Ado about Nothing,* Act V, Scene 1 (WS)
2   *Ten Years' Exile,* Madame de Staël
3   *Essays,* Intellect (RWE)
4   *Representative Men,* Plato; or the Philosopher (RWE)

This remains the case. Astrophysicists know much about the history of the universe but they don't know why there is one. Another mystery is the mind—the being of humans.

> The philosophy of six thousand years has not searched the chambers and magazines of the soul. In its experiments there has always remained, in the last analysis, a residuum it could not resolve. Man is a stream whose source is hidden.[1]

There remains the humbling uncertainty—the recognition that our understanding has limits.

> People disparage knowing and the intellectual life, and urge doing. I am very content with knowing, if only I could know.[2]

Animals live their lives within limited spheres of understanding—and so must we.

> Illusion, Temperament, Succession, Surface, Surprise, Reality, Subjectiveness, — these are threads on the loom of time, these are the lords of life. I dare not assume to give their order, but I name them as I find them in my way. I know better than to claim any completeness for my picture. I am a fragment, and this is a fragment of me.[3]

Emerson had his own cheering philosophic faith.

> All our progress is an unfolding, like the vegetable bud. You have first an instinct, then an opinion, then a knowledge, as the plant has root, bud, and fruit. Trust the instinct to the end, though you can render no reason. It is vain to hurry it.[4]

> It is not in an arbitrary "decree of God," but in the nature of man that a veil shuts down on the facts of tomorrow: for the soul will not have us read any

---

1   *Essays,* The Over-soul (RWE)
2   *Essays: Second Series,* Experience (RWE)
3   *Essays: Second Series,* Experience (RWE)
4   *Essays,* Intellect (RWE)

other cipher but that of cause and effect. By this
veil, which curtains events, it instructs the children
of men to live in today. The only mode of obtaining
an answer to these questions of the senses, is,
to forego all low curiosity, and, accepting the tide
of being which floats us into the secret of nature,
work and live, work and live, and all unawares, the
advancing soul has built and forged for itself a new
condition, and the question and the answer are
one.[1]

Emerson enjoined us to "work and live." Freud said, "love and work."

Emerson realized the importance of scientific knowledge to human beings. From progress to date he drew remarkable extrapolations!

Geology has initiated us into the secularity
of nature, and taught us to disuse our dame-
school measures, and exchange our Mosaic and
Ptolemaic schemes for her large style. We knew
nothing rightly, for want of perspective. Now we
learn what patient periods must round themselves
before the rock is formed, then before the rock is
broken, and the first lichen race has disintegrated
the thinnest external plate into soil, and opened
the door for the remote Flora, Fauna, Ceres,
and Pomona, to come in. How far off yet is the
trilobite! how far the quadruped! how inconceivably
remote is man! All duly arrive, and then race after
race of men. It is a long way from granite to the
oyster; farther yet to Plato, and the preaching of
the immortality of the soul. Yet all must come, as
surely as the first atom has two sides.[2]

In the paragraph above, published in 1844, fifteen years before *Origin of Species*, Emerson anticipated part of the theory of evolution. In the following he seems to speak of a universe-igniting big bang.

---

1   *Essays,* The Over-soul (RWE)
2   *Essays: Second Series,* Nature (RWE)

> It was no great affair, a mere push, but the
> astronomers were right in making much of it,
> for there is no end to the consequences of the
> act. That famous aboriginal push propagates
> itself through all the balls of the system, and
> through every atom of every ball, through all the
> races of creatures, and through the history and
> performances of every individual.[1]

Although it would be a stretch to say that Emerson anticipated quantum theory, his statement about duality is suggestive.

> The end and the means, the gamester and the
> game, — life is made up of the intermixture and
> reaction of these two amicable powers, whose
> marriage appears beforehand monstrous, as each
> denies and tends to abolish the other. We must
> reconcile the contradictions as we can, but their
> discord and their concord introduce wild absurdities
> into our thinking and speech. No sentence will hold
> the whole truth, and the only way in which we can
> be just, is by giving ourselves the lie; Speech is
> better than silence; silence is better than speech; —
> All things are in contact; every atom has a sphere of
> repulsion; — Things are, and are not, at the same
> time; — and the like. All the universe over, there is
> but one thing, this old Two-Face, creator-creature,
> mind-matter, right-wrong, of which any proposition
> may be affirmed or Denied.[2]

In the end, Emerson felt that his mission of thought took him beyond science. Science was all very well as far as it went, but his quest was in a different realm.

> The motive of science was the extension of man,
> on all sides, into Nature, till his hands should touch
> the stars, his eyes see through the earth, his ears
> understand the language of beast and bird, and

---

1 *Essays: Second Series,* Nature (RWE)
2 *Essays: Second Series,* Nominalist and Realist (RWE)

the sense of the wind; and, through his sympathy, heaven and earth should talk with him. But that is not our science. These geologies, chemistries, astronomies, seem to make wise, but they leave us where they found us.[1]

The human heart concerns us more than the poring into microscopes, and is larger than can be measured by the pompous figures of the astronomer.[2]

Emerson could set science beyond the plane of his focus, but learning and institutions for learning—education—were close to home and had to be reckoned with. Learning is indispensable. Ignorance imposes limitations.

College education is the reading of certain books which the common sense of all scholars agrees will represent the science already accumulated. If you know that, — for instance in geometry, if you have read Euclid and Laplace, — your opinion has some value; if you do not know these, you are not entitled to give any opinion on the subject.[3]

Liberal education qualifies a person for membership in knowledge-based conversation. But it does not make you a world-changer.

Not out of those, on whom systems of education have exhausted their culture, comes the helpful giant to destroy the old or to build the new, but out of unhandselled savage nature, out of terrible Druids and Berserkirs, come at last Alfred and Shakespeare.[4]

Emerson saw another limitation of schooling.

---

1 *Conduct of Life,* Beauty (RWE)
2 *Conduct of Life,* Beauty (RWE)
3 *Society and Solitude,* Books (RWE)
4 *Addresses,* The American Scholar (RWE)

> The boy believes there is a teacher who can sell
> him wisdom.[1]

So also hoped those who paid to hear Emerson's lectures and who bought his books.

Experience

The Transcendentalists emphasized the value of sensory experience in the natural world. Emerson sounded this theme in memorable language in his first book.

> The lover of nature is he whose inward and outward
> senses are still truly adjusted to each other; who
> has retained the spirit of infancy even into the era
> of manhood. His intercourse with heaven and earth,
> becomes part of his daily food. In the presence of
> nature, a wild delight runs through the man, in spite
> of real sorrows. Nature says,—he is my creature,
> and maugre all his impertinent griefs, he shall be
> glad with me. Not the sun or the summer alone,
> but every hour and season yields its tribute of
> delight; for every hour and change corresponds to
> and authorizes a different state of the mind, from
> breathless noon to grimmest midnight. Nature is a
> setting that fits equally well a comic or a mourning
> piece. In good health, the air is a cordial of
> incredible virtue.[2]

> Nature never became a toy to a wise spirit. The
> flowers, the animals, the mountains, reflected the
> wisdom of his best hour, as much as they had
> delighted the simplicity of his childhood.[3]

In *As You Like It,* Shakespeare's protagonist, the exiled duke makes this observation to the group that has joined him in living outdoors.

---

1   *Representative Men,* Uses of Great Men (RWE)
2   *Nature,* Chapter 1. Nature (RWE)
3   *Nature,* Chapter 1. Nature (RWE)

> Sweet are the uses of adversity,
> Which, like the toad, ugly and venomous,
> Wears yet a precious jewel in his head;
> And this our life, exempt from public haunt,
> Finds tongues in trees, books in the running brooks,
> Sermons in stones, and good in everything.[1]

Social and cultural experiences are also important. Emerson thought they reduced self-absorption.

> The antidotes against this organic egotism, are,
> the range and variety of attractions, as gained by
> acquaintance with the world, with men of merit, with
> classes of society, with travel, with eminent persons,
> and with the high resources of philosophy, art, and
> religion: books, travel, society, solitude.[2]

Carl Rogers wrote,

> I have come to have more respect for those vague
> thoughts which occur in me from time to time, which
> *feel* as though they were significant. I think of it as
> trusting the totality of my experience, which I have
> learned to suspect is wiser than my intellect. It is
> fallible I am sure, but I believe it to be less fallible
> than my conscious mind alone.[3]

Here's how Emerson expressed that idea.

> Experience is, for me, the highest authority. The
> touchstone of validity is my own experience.
> Be true to your own act, and congratulate yourself if
> you have done something strange and extravagant,
> and broken the monotony of a decorous age.[4]

Time

Time is unique among the resources of living beings. The judicious use of time determines success or failure. Were a

---

1   *As You Like It,* Act II, Scene 1 (WS)
2   *Conduct of Life,* Culture (RWE)
3   *On Becoming a Person,* Carl Rogers
4   *Essays,* Culture (RWE)

bluebird to skimp on her nest, in haste to lay her eggs, she would find it impossible to manage their temperature. But if she fusses forever to make her nest perfect, her young will not mature by autumn. Michaelangelo must have given a lot of thought to the shape he wished to give his David, but, in the end, he had to hack the marble.

> Time, which shows so vacant, indivisible and divine in its coming, is slit and peddled into trifles and tatters. A door is to be painted, a lock to be repaired. I want wood, or oil, or meal, or salt; the house smokes, or I have a head ache; then the tax; and an affair to be transacted with a man without heart or brains; and the stinging recollection of an injurious or very awkward word, these eat up the hours.[1]

Emerson's regret at the day's hours being *slit and peddled into trifles and tatters* was expanded in a later work.

> The shortest enumeration of our wants in this rugged climate appalls us by the multitude of things not easy to be done. And if you look at the multitude of particulars, one would say: Good housekeeping is impossible; order is too precious a thing to dwell with men and women. See, in families where there is both substance and taste, at what expense any favorite punctuality is maintained. If the children, for example, are considered, dressed, dieted, attended, kept in proper company, schooled, and at home fostered by the parents, — then does the hospitality of the house suffer; friends are less carefully bestowed, the daily table less catered. If the hours of meals are punctual, the apartments are slovenly. If the linens and hangings are clean and fine, and the furniture good, the yard, the garden, the fences are neglected. If all are well attended; then must the master and mistress be studious of particulars at the cost of their own

---

1   *Essays,* Prudence (RWE)

accomplishments and growth, — or persons are
treated as things.[1]

A poor Indian chief of the Six Nations of New York
made a wiser reply than any philosopher, to some
one complaining that he had not enough time.
"Well," said Red Jacket, "I suppose you have all
there is."[2]

On the subject of time and timing, Shakespeare wrote,

There is a tide in the affairs of men,
Which, taken at the flood, leads on to fortune;
Omitted, all the voyage of their life is bound in
shallows and in miseries.
On such a full sea are we now afloat;
And we must take the current when it serves,
Or lose our ventures.[3]

Thus spoke Shakespeare's Romans. His English characters
are less formal, as when Henry, the crown prince, rebukes his
recent drinking companion.

Falstaff. Now, Hal, what time of day is it, lad?
Henry V. Thou art so fat-witted, with drinking of
old sack and unbuttoning thee after supper and
sleeping upon benches after noon, that thou hast
forgotten to demand that truly which thou wouldst
truly know. What a devil hast thou to do with the
time of the day? Unless hours were cups of sack
and clocks the tongues of bawds and the blessed
sun himself a fair hot wench, I see no reason why
thou shouldst be so superfluous to demand the
time of the day.[4]

Later, Henry's rival, Hotspur, chides his co-conspirators,

O gentlemen, the time of life is short!

---

1   *Society and Solitude,* Domestic Life (RWE)
2   *Society and Solitude,* Works and Days (RWE)
3   *Julius Caesar,* Act IV, Scene 3 (WS)
4   *Henry IV Part I,* Act I, Scene 2 (WS)

To spend that shortness basely were too long.[1]

In our culture, one proper use of time is to get work done.

> The high prize of life, the crowning fortune of a man
> is to be born with a bias to some pursuit, which
> finds him in employment and happiness, — whether
> it be to make baskets, or broadswords, or canals,
> or statutes, or songs.[2]

To end the chapter where it began,

> We have a pretty artillery of tools now in our social
> arrangements: we ride four times as fast as our
> fathers did; travel, grind, weave, forge, plant, till,
> and excavate better. We have new shoes, gloves,
> glasses, an gimlets; we have the calculus; we have
> the newspaper, which does its best to make every
> square acre of land and sea give an account of
> itself at your breakfast-table; we have money, and
> paper money; we have language, — the finest tool
> of all, and nearest to the mind.[3]

---

1 *Henry IV Part I*, Act V, Scene 2 (WS)
2 *Conduct of Life*, Considerations by the Way (RWE)
3 *Society and Solitude*, Works and Days (RWE)

Conclusion

What has *not* changed since the days of Emerson, Fuller, and Whitman? Our usage of the word character, as it refers to desirable personal qualities, has held constant. Individuals with good character are genuine, meaning that they wear the same face; they show no masks, and they are reliable. They are grounded; their internal perceptions align well with the real world. They are gracious; they pay attention to the feelings and comfort of others. People with good character do their best to discern and support fair play—they try to see points of view unlike their own. In my reading of their work, our authors would accept these criteria for good character. Strength of character is the readiness to maintain these qualities in adverse circumstances and the courage to express ideals in words and actions.

The fundamental challenges of being a person have also been stable over time. We face the same dilemmas and embody the same contradictions as our thoughtful forebearers. We need bonds of care with family and friends, and cherish them, but in important respects our aloneness is final. Our pride in doing good work lifts our spirits—but we wonder, at times, how much it matters—our inner Falstaff mocks our ambitions. We want to speak honestly but we don't want to hurt anyone's feelings. We feel sympathy with the sufferings of others—but to live cheerfully, for the welfare of ourselves and of those around us, we must insulate ourselves to some extent. We desire to live in, and savor, the present moment—but our thoughts race ahead to choices, contingencies, and plans— the mental activities that bring success in every realm. And, perhaps more than ever, the search for meaning traverses a slippery slope.

Human nature has not changed—but our circumstances are different. Science and technology continue to deepen our knowledge of cause and effect, increasing our life-saving powers of prediction and action. It has become far easier to obtain information—a power that grows geometrically. Society has become more accepting of individual differences. The former prejudice against groups other than straight white men has, at least in some circles, gone out of favor. Bigoted reactions might be felt but they may no longer be expressed with impunity. Family structure is more fluid, with greater acceptance of divorce, remarriage, and unmarried domestic partnerships. Perhaps this has its costs but it allows people more latitude in being who they are, rolling back barriers to unfolding of self. You can be elected to high office although female or gay or of color. In their own time, the Transcendentalists' love of nature could not stop Americans from plundering natural resources. A perceived obligation to steward our Earth has grown slowly. These improvements are partial and they are subject to retrograde swings of the cultural pendulum—but there has been real change.

Do people now live at a higher ethical level? Have fairness and kindness increased? Do people, on average, treat each other with greater respect and tenderness than formerly? In my best guess, they do, somewhat. I attribute the change to the partial realization of Margaret Fuller's vision of equality of the sexes. Women tend to be more empathic than men. The increased social power of women releases kindness from men that was formerly repressed by primitive notions of masculinity. This has accomplished a change in manners. Expressions of prejudice have become impolite. Your hatreds reflect poorly on yourself. The change in these permissions is indistinguishable from an improvement in the general ethical standard.

What actions, what choices, elevate our characters? Attention to the arts, especially to literature, increases groundedness by exposing us to viewpoints other than our own. These vicarious experiences are an aid to recognizing fairness. Careful selection of companions makes it easier for us to be gracious and genuine, although those two aspirations are ever in tension. Sweetness of manner is apt to sound insincere. Graciousness aims for Cordelia's blend of care and candor, precisely expressed. Attentive parents try to help their children articulate their feelings. Adults work on their own powers of expression through writing, conversation, and talk therapy.

We become kinder by observing and imitating models of kindness in our lives. The blessing of such models is unevenly distributed—a lamentable reality. Enlightened children's media tries to help, but families have the strongest influence.

The exercise of character requires us to balance humility and confidence, empathy and cheerfulness, kindness and candor, self-acceptance and self-criticism. Ambitious work mustn't preclude attention to family, friends, and community. Emerson found it challenging to juggle all this, and so do we. Continual adjustments are required, giving rise to frequent doubts that we're getting it right. Remember Whitman's encouragement:

> The hopples fall from your ankles, you find an
> unfailing sufficiency,
>   Old or young, male or female, rude, low, rejected
> by the rest,
>   whatever you are promulges itself,
>   Through birth, life, death, burial, the means are
> provided, nothing
>   is scanted,
>   Through angers, losses, ambition, ignorance,
> ennui, what you are
> picks its way.[1]

---

1   *Leaves of Grass,* You (WW)

Bibliography

Austen, Jane. *Pride and Prejudice*. New York: Knopf, 1991.

Buell, Lawrence. *Emerson*. Cambridge, MA: Harvard University Press, 2003.

Cabot, James Elliot. *A Memoir of Ralph Waldo Emerson*. Boston: Houghton, Mifflin and Company, 1887.

Child, Lydia Maria. *Letters of Lydia Maria Child*. Boston and New York: Houghton, Mifflin and Co., 1883.

Cross, Wilbur L. and Tucker Brooke, eds. *The Yale Shakespeare*. New York: Barnes and Noble, 1993.

Emerson, Edward Waldo. *Emerson in Concord; A Memoir*. Boston: Houghton, Mifflin and Company, The Riverside Press, 1895.

Emerson, Ralph Waldo. *The Complete Works of Ralph Waldo Emerson*. Boston: Houghton, Mifflin and Company, The Riverside Press, 1876. (Original publication dates of the books cited here are: *Nature*, 1836, *ssays, 1841, Essays: Second Series*, 1844, *Representative Men*, 1849, *English Traits*, 1856, *The Conduct of Life*, 1860, *Society and Solitude*, 1870. Addresses cited are "The American Scholar" (1837), "The Divinity School Address" (1838), "Literary Ethics" (1838), "Man the Reformer" (1841), "Lecture on the Times" (1841), and "Method of Nature," (1841).

Fuller, Margaret Ossoli. *Woman in the Nineteenth Century, and Kindred Papers relating to the Sphere, Condition, and Duties of Woman*. Westport, CT: Greenwood Press, 1977. Originally published Boston: Roberts Brothers, 1874.

Goodwin, Joan W. *The Remarkable Mrs. Ripley: The Life of Sarah Alden Bradford Ripley*. Boston: Northeastern University Press, Hanover, NH: University Press of New England, 1998.

Holmes, Oliver Wendell. *Ralph Walo Emerson*. Boston: Houghton, Mifflin and Company, 1895.

Kuhn, Thomas S. *The Copernican Revolution: Planetary Astronomy in the Development of Western Thought.* Cambridge, MA: Harvard University Press, 1957.

Madame de Staël. *Madame de Staël on Politics, Literature, and National Character.* Garden City, NY: Doubleday, 1964.

Madame de Staël. *Ten Years' Exile: Memoirs of That Interesting Period of the Life of the Baroness De Staël-Holstein, Written by Herself, during the Years 1810, 1811, 1812, and 1813, and Now First Published from the Original Manuscript, by Her Son.* Project Gutenberg.

Marcus, James. *Glad to the Brink of Fear: A Portrait of Ralph Waldo Emerson,* Princeton, NJ: Princeton University Press, 2024.

Marshall, Megan. *Margaret Fuller, A New American Life.* Boston: Houghton Mifflin Harcourt, 2013.

Meltzer, Milton, and Holland, Patricia G., eds. *Lydia Maria Child: Selected Letters, 1817-1880.* Amherst: The University of Massachusetts Press, Amherst, 1982.

Miller, Perry, ed. *The Transcentalists.* Cambridge, MA: Harvard University Press, 1950.

Rogers, Carl. *On Becoming a Person: A Therapist's View of Psychotherapy.* Boston: Houghton Mifflin, Boston. 1961.

Sandburg, Carl. *The Complete Poems of Carl Sandburg.* New York: Harcourt Brace Jovanovich, 1970.

Shakespeare, William. *The Complete Plays of William Shakespeare.* Project Gutenberg. https://www.gutenberg.org/ebooks/100

Shakespeare, William. *The Yale Shakespeare.* New York: Barnes & Noble Books, 1993.

Whitman, Walt. *Leaves of Grass.* New York: Barnes and Noble, 1993.

A Note from the Editor

The process that led to this book began with reading Emerson's essays and noting passages about topics concerning the philosophy of everyday life. I wondered what Shakespeare, in his plays, might have to say about the same topics, so I read those, too. Continuing to feel rewarded by this undertaking, I went on to Walt Whitman's *Leaves of Grass* and to the works of Madame de Staël and Margaret Fuller.

Preparing adult education classes to discuss these topics required placing them in groups and giving them a sequence. Doing so opened the way to adding comments and publishing this volume. I am grateful to the individuals who enrolled in the classes; I gained much from our conversations.

My gratitude and appreciation extend to Katrina Kelner and Larry Buell, whose suggestions improved the text, to Jaimee Joroff, for her encouragement and her suggestion about the cover, and to my wife, Betsy Stokey, who creates an atmosphere in which sustained effort is possible.